The United States and a Rising China

Strategic and Military Implications

Zalmay M. Khalilzad, Abram N. Shulsky,
Daniel L. Byman, Roger Cliff, David T. Orletsky,
David Shlapak, Ashley J. Tellis

PREPARED FOR THE UNITED STATES AIR FORCE

Project AIR FORCE

RAND

This report summarizes the findings of a multiyear project entitled "Chinese Defense Modernization and Its Implications for the United States Air Force." It focuses on the fundamental question of how U.S. policy should deal with China, a rising power that could have the capability, in the not too distant future, of challenging the U.S. position in East Asia and U.S. military, political, and economic access to that dynamic and important region. It then specifically addresses the implications for the U.S. Air Force (USAF), in the areas of shaping the environment, deterrence and warfighting. This summary draws heavily on the other work conducted in the course of the study. The results of some of this work have been, or will soon be, published in other RAND documents.

This project is being conducted in the Strategy and Doctrine Program of Project AIR FORCE under the sponsorship of the Deputy Chief of Staff for Air and Space Operations, U.S. Air Force (AF/XO) and the Commander, Pacific Air Forces (PACAF/CC). This report should be of interest to members of the national security community and to interested members of the general public. Comments are welcomed and may be addressed to the project leader, Dr. Zalmay Khalilzad.

PROJECT AIR FORCE

Project AIR FORCE, a division of RAND, is the Air Force federally funded research and development center (FFRDC) for studies and analyses. It provides the Air Force with independent analyses of policy alternatives affecting the development, employment, combat readiness, and support of current and future aerospace forces.

Research is performed in four programs: Aerospace Force Development; Manpower, Personnel, and Training; Resource Management; and Strategy and Doctrine

CONTENTS

FIGURE AND TABLES

Figure

Table

SUMMARY

Since 1978, China has been embarked on a fundamental process of reform and modernization that has resulted in an unprecedented rate of economic development. Some analysts predict that this will enable China's gross national product to overtake that of the United States in the early part of the next century. Although China currently lags far behind the United States militarily and technologically, a robust Chinese economy will likely be capable of underwriting rapid and dramatic improvements in these areas as well.

This report discusses the major issues China's modernization raises for the United States. It looks at how China is likely to behave in world affairs and the challenges that behavior may pose, what strategy the United States should follow to deal with those challenges, and how the China factor should inform U.S. political-military activities in the East Asian region.

DETERMINANTS OF CHINESE BEHAVIOR

At present, the most important determinant of China's foreign-policy behavior is its pursuit of "comprehensive national power." The goal is to make China a developed country, which would have the effect of, among other things, raising the standard of living of the population and preparing the technological-industrial base for a strong military. In pursuit of modernization, the leadership has relaxed its internal controls over the population and has opened the country to foreign influences. In addition, the Chinese leadership has recognized that good relations with the United States are strongly advisable, if not absolutely necessary, for the success of its pursuit of "comprehensive national power." However, two other drivers of Chinese policy—concern for sovereignty (e.g., eventual reunification with Taiwan) and regime maintenance (i.e., the maintenance of Communist Party rule)—place important limitations on the extent to which China's desire for good relations with the United States will determine its behavior.

Once China becomes fully modern or advanced (something which is hard to imagine happening before 2050), it could become a major rival for world power.[1] But before that, China could prove a difficult military adversary in East Asia, a region of vital importance to the United States. A militarily and economically strong China might also offer an alternative to the current U.S. role as the region's preferred security partner and its ultimate security manager. A China that approached or equaled the United States in power would presumably seek to vindicate its territorial claims and could strive to attain regional hegemony, increase its status in global terms, and alter the rules of the international system to its advantage. Both realist theory and the Chinese tradition of belief in its own geopolitical centrality in Asia would suggest such a result. Four developments, however, could lessen the prospects for such a negative outcome:

First, the Chinese leadership could retain its current emphasis on the importance of good relations with the United States even as the country successfully modernizes. For one thing, the modernization process will not have a clear-cut endpoint; even after several decades of successful economic and technological development, China will likely be behind the United States in many respects, and the leadership may still feel the need to "catch up." More fundamentally, the dynamism of technology and the global economy is such that even the most advanced countries quickly find that they must remain open to each other if they wish to keep pace; no country is able on its own to develop all relevant technologies to world-class standards. Hence, no country can cut itself off from the rest of the world without quickly falling behind.

---

[1]This assumes that China retains an authoritarian form of government or that, as it democratizes, chauvinist sentiments (among the populace and/or the elites) play a large role in determining foreign policy.

Second, and most optimistically, the Chinese leadership could undergo an "acculturation" process, by which it becomes more and more willing to abide by the general norms of the current international system. Thus, this theory goes, although China's current acquiescence in these norms may be tentative and "insincere," driven solely by the need for foreign contributions to China's modernization, the leadership will gradually come to understand that these norms can serve China's interests as well. By the time China becomes strong enough to challenge the current international order, it will have become reconciled to it.

Third, the opening of China to the world, the relaxation of restrictions on travel and communication and the rapid growth of an educated middle class raise the possibility of a transformation of the communist regime in the direction of more democracy. Although the process of democratization could produce aggressive external behavior, the attainment of democracy can be expected, based on the experience of other democracies, to lead China to adopt a generally cooperative strategy.

Fourth, because of any of a number of difficulties in the economic, social and political realms, China could face chaos or collapse, which would reduce its ability to mount a major challenge to the United States, although it could lead to other problems. It is possible that a failing regime would be tempted to undertake aggressive external policies to gain increased domestic legitimacy. Alternatively, a weak regime might become more inward-looking and be less focused on, and/or less capable of, vindicating its claims to Taiwan or the South China Sea. In any case, a chaotic China could become a source of refugee flows that could threaten to swamp neighboring countries or that could encourage non-Han populations in China to seek independence.

CHINESE MILITARY IN TRANSITION

Military modernization is an important Chinese goal. However, China has been pursuing this objective as a long-term strategic program as opposed to an urgent requirement. China does not want to do what the Soviet Union did, i.e., place an unbearable burden on its economy by spending too much on its military forces. But it also does not intend to follow Japan in limiting its military capabilities to a level far below what its economy could support.

Although China today has the world's largest armed forces, it is indisputably not a "peer competitor" of the United States. Nevertheless, the current Chinese military possesses four important characteristics that differentiate it from the adversaries in the "standard" major theater war (MTW) planning cases, such as Iraq and North Korea:

- China has nuclear weapons that can reach U.S. territory.

- The People's Liberation Army (PLA) fields a variety of surface-to-surface missiles that would prove especially problematic for current and near-term future U.S. ballistic missile defenses.

- The absolute size of the PLA would present challenges.

- China's geographic extent may make it very difficult for U.S. forces to reach and attack the full range of targets that the U.S. military would anticipate striking in the course of an MTW.

Thus, even today's PLA—ponderous, poorly trained, and ill-equipped as it is—presents unique and more demanding planning and operational challenges to U.S. strategists contemplating a possible confrontation with China.[2] However, China recognizes its military weaknesses and has embarked on a sustained two-tracked approach to modernizing the PLA—arms purchases from abroad and indigenous development—which, if sustained through the first several decades, would greatly intensify those challenges. Indigenous development is also facilitated by espionage (theft of technology and/or plans for weapon systems), as well as by the covert acquisition abroad of export-controlled components, manufacturing equipment, and other technology.

Given current trends, China could emerge, by 2015, as a formidable power, one that might be labeled a *multidimensional regional competitor*. Such a China could credibly

- exercise sea denial with respect to the seas contiguous to China

- contest aerospace superiority in a sustained way in areas contiguous to China's borders

---

[2]This, of course, should not be read as a *prediction* that such a conflict will occur.

- threaten U.S. operating locations in East Asia with a variety of long-range strike assets
- challenge U.S. information dominance
- pose a strategic nuclear threat to the United States.

U.S. POLICY TOWARD CHINA

Given the potential for both positive and negative developments with regard to Chinese behavior, what U.S. policies are most appropriate? The fundamental U.S. policy toward China has been one of "engagement," which seeks to maintain and enhance relations with China as much as possible in the various policy realms. Engagement rests on the assumption that continued contact affects Chinese behavior in a positive direction and produces economic benefits for the United States. In the meantime, however, it helps China develop economically and technologically: Hence, if engagement does not lead to more cooperative Chinese behavior, it may have helped China become a potentially more threatening adversary in the future.

Some have suggested that containment would be a more realistic way to deal with the prospect of a powerful China in the future. However, containment would be a very difficult policy to implement: First, it would be hard to obtain a domestic consensus to subordinate other policy goals (including trade and investment) to dealing with a Chinese threat that is as yet, to say the least, far from manifest. Second, containment would require, to be effective, the whole-hearted cooperation of regional allies and most of the other advanced industrial countries of the world; again, such cooperation would be difficult to obtain. In general, containment seems to accept as fated something that does not appear to be inevitable; seems unnecessarily to resign itself to an unfavorable outcome, while overlooking the possibility that Sino-U.S. relations could evolve in a more cooperative direction; and would create a confrontation where none existed.

Given the difficulties surrounding both containment and engagement, a combination of the two policies appears, for the present, to have the best chance of preserving the hopeful potential of the engagement policy while hedging against its possible inability to avert a future Chinese challenge to U.S interests and objectives.

Such a "third way" policy would continue to try to bring China into the current international system while both preparing for a possible Chinese challenge to it and seeking to convince the Chinese leadership that a challenge would be difficult and extremely risky to pursue. The elements of such a policy would be

- **Modified Engagement.** This policy would modify current engagement by being less solicitous of Chinese sensitivities on such issues as human rights and by making a greater effort to impose sanctions on specific Chinese companies that, for example, exported sensitive nuclear materials, violated U.S. export control laws, or otherwise thwarted major U.S. objectives.

- **Strengthening of Ties to Regional Countries.** The United States would seek to strengthen its ties to regional countries so as to be in a better position to enable them to resist any possible future Chinese aggression. Steps should include promoting improved relations among East Asian states so as to facilitate their cooperation on security issues in the future should China become hostile. This would be aimed at emphasizing to China the costs of, and thereby deterring, any Chinese attempt at seeking regional hegemony.

- **Dealing with the Taiwan Issue.** The United States would emphasize the importance of a peaceful resolution of the Taiwan issue and would help the Taiwanese preserve the *status quo* for as long as uncertainty about China's future course endures. Should China evolve in a democratic and friendly direction, U.S. policy could shift toward one of encouragement and support for voluntary reunification; if China became fundamentally hostile, the United States could support a strengthening of Taiwan's *de facto* independent status.

Should a more-powerful China push for regional hegemony or attack Taiwan, the "third way" policy could be turned into containment. But should China become democratic and cooperative, this "engage and hedge" policy would give way to a partnership between the two countries.

IMPLICATIONS FOR THE U.S. MILITARY AND THE USAF IN PARTICULAR

The "third way" policy has important implications for the future of U.S. military forces. These may be considered under the three headings of shaping the political-military environment, deterrence, and warfighting.

The main shaping role the U.S. armed forces play is to maintain overall military superiority and the specific ability to defeat threats to vital interests from a potentially hostile China. However, as part of a policy of engagement, the USAF, as well as the rest of the U.S. armed forces, has a role to play in conducting military-to-military contacts with the PLA. Such contacts can help shape China's strategic perceptions; strengthen deterrence; increase transparency; and, by developing personal ties between officers on both sides, provide a valuable informal communications mechanism that can be useful on a day-to-day basis and could prove vital in time of crisis.

In addition to conducting military-to-military contacts, the U.S. armed forces must be able to deter China from taking steps contrary to U.S. interests. In some cases, that will involve demonstrating an evident ability to prevent China from attaining its goals via the use of force. Historically, it has been difficult to deter China from taking a wide range of undesirable actions, especially when they have been designed more for their political than their military effects. To deter China, even those who were more powerful have had to threaten high levels of violence.

Ultimately, of course, U.S. armed forces must be prepared to defeat China militarily if it threatens vital U.S. interests. Chinese military modernization poses many potential challenges for the U.S. armed forces, and the USAF in particular, as they seek to maintain a margin of military superiority over China. Among the most important implications for the USAF are

- **Dealing with the Potential Threat of Chinese Nuclear, Biological, and Chemical Weapons and Missiles.** The U.S. military, including the USAF, should seek to provide defenses against ballistic and cruise missiles. The USAF should place increased emphasis on longer-range platforms that could be based outside the range of most future Chinese attack systems.

- **Assuring Air Superiority.** The USAF should continue to field aircraft and munitions with low-observable ("stealth") characteristics and reevaluate the planned purchases of next-generation munitions as planned numbers may be insufficient to wage an effective campaign against a modernized PLA.

- **Protecting U.S. Space and Information Systems.** The Chinese, perceiving themselves to be far less dependent on space than the United States, could consider initiating a counter-space campaign. The Chinese might also seek to disrupt U.S. ability to respond to their aggression by attacking U.S. information systems.

- **Ensuring Access to the Theater.** The USAF should consider options for improving access to the Western Pacific. Besides ensuring continued access to Japanese and Korean bases even after Korean unification or reconciliation, the United States should place a greater emphasis on Southeast Asia to enable it to respond to contingencies in that region and the South China Sea as well.

- **Putting Greater Emphasis on Longer-Range Systems.** The current force mix is dominated by short-legged systems. Given the distances involved in the Pacific, the USAF should review its modernization plans for the middle term and consider changes that would emphasize longer range systems such as medium range bombers and stand-off long range (cruise or ballistic) missiles and, over the very long term, space-based systems.

ACKNOWLEDGMENTS

Project AIR FORCE's work on "Chinese Military Modernization and Its Implications for the United States Air Force," whose results this report summarizes, could not have been conducted without the strong and loyal support of its sponsors, Gen John Jumper, former Deputy Chief of Staff, Plans and Operations; Gen Patrick Gamble, Commander, Pacific Air Forces and former Deputy Chief of Staff, Air and Space Operations; Gen John Lorber, former Commander, Pacific Air Forces; Gen Richard Myers, former Commander, Pacific Air Forces; Lt Gen Marvin Esmond, Deputy Chief of Staff, Air and Space Operations; and Maj Gen John Casciano, Director, Intelligence, Surveillance and Reconnaissance. We are very grateful to them for their continuing faith and interest in our work.

Our action officers, majors Mark Stokes, Steve Cunico, and Milton Johnson; Capt Rod Erickson; and James Hertsch have been very helpful in opening doors for us and helping ensure our work's relevance to the concerns of the senior USAF leadership.

During the course of this project, we were most fortunate to have the opportunity to brief many current and former senior officials and to receive their valuable comments, suggestions, and critiques of our work in progress. We are particularly grateful to them for the time and effort they were willing to expend in this manner. This illustrious group included Gen Michael Ryan, Chief of Staff of the Air Force; Gen Ralph Eberhart, Vice Chief of Staff of the Air Force; ADM Joseph Prueher, Commander-in-Chief, Pacific Command; Andrew W. Marshall, Director of Net Assessment, Office of the Secretary of Defense; former Secretaries of Defense Harold Brown, Frank

Carlucci, and William Perry, former Chairman of the Joint Chiefs of Staff John Shalikashvili; and former Advisor to the President for National Security Affairs Brent Scowcroft.

RAND colleagues Mark Burles, Brian G. Chow, Greg Jones, and James Mulvenon were members of the project team who contributed to all phases of the effort. They enhanced the project's work with contributions on such subjects as China's relations with Central Asia, Chinese nuclear and ballistic missile programs, and information warfare. Since their contributions were not directly included in this overview report, they are not listed on the title page; however, they were full participants in the project, as much as those whose names appear as authors.

Seven RAND military fellows made important contributions to the work of the project, and we wish to acknowledge their efforts here: CAPT James Droddy, USN; CAPT Nicholas Trongale, USN; CDR Nelson Cayabyab, USN; LtCol. Brian Dingess, USMC; Lt Col Barbara Kuennecke, USAF; Lt Col Daniel McCusker, USAF; and CDR Bruce Woodyard, USN. Commander Cayabyab and Lieutenant Colonel Dingess also prepared classified reports as part of the overall project.

I. Lewis Libby and David Shambaugh reviewed an earlier version of this work and provided many useful comments and suggestions. Phyllis Gilmore did yeoman work in editing the manuscript. In addition, we wish to thank our research assistants, Toshi Yoshihara and Andrew Mok, for their diligence; Susan Spindel for her able secretarial support; and, last but not least, our secretary, Luetta Pope, for her patience, hard work, and demonstrated ability to roll with the many punches that came her way in the course of this project.

GLOSSARY

ACDA	U.S. Arms Control and Disarmament Agency
AMRAAM	Advanced Medium-Range Air-to-Air Missile
ARF	ASEAN Regional Forum
ASEAN	Association of Southeast Asian Nations
ASW	Antisubmarine warfare
AWACS	Airborne Warning and Control System
BMD	Ballistic Missile Defense
CRAF	Civil Reserve Air Fleet
DF	*Dongfeng* [East Wind]—used with a number (e.g., DF-5) to designate a specific type of Chinese land-based ballistic missile
DPP	Democratic Progressive Party [Taiwan]
EROS	Earth Resources Observation Satellite
FEER	*Far Eastern Economic Review*
FSW	A Chinese photoreconnaissance satellite type
GDP	Gross domestic product
GLONASS	A Russian satellite system similar to the U.S. GPS
GNP	Gross national product
GPS	Global Positioning System

ICBM	Intercontinental ballistic missile
IISS	International Institute for Strategic Studies
IRBM	Intermediate-range ballistic missile
JL	*Ju Lang* [Giant Wave]—used with a number (e.g., JL-1) to designate a specific type of Chinese SLBM
KILO	Class of Soviet conventional attack submarine
LANDSAT	Land Remote Satellite Sensing System
MFN	Most-favored nation
MiG	Used with a number (e.g., MiG-21) to designate a Soviet fighter type
MIRV	Multiple independently targetable reentry vehicle
MRBM	Medium-range ballistic missile
MTW	Major theater war
NBC	Nuclear, biological, and chemical
PLA	People's Liberation Army
PLAAF	People's Liberation Army Air Force
PLAN	People's Liberation Army Navy
PRC	People's Republic of China
R&D	Research and development
RADARSAT	Radar Satellite [Canada]
RMB	Renminbei
SAM	Surface-to-air missile
SLBM	Submarine-launched ballistic missile
SOEs	State-owned enterprises
SPOT	*Satellite pour l'Observation de la Terre* (French commercial photoreconnaissance satellite)
SRBM	Short-range ballistic missile

SSBN	Nuclear ballistic-missile submarine
SSN	Nuclear attack submarine
USAF	U.S. Air Force
WTO	World Trade Organization
XXJ	A Chinese fighter in development

Chapter One

INTRODUCTION

Since 1978, China has been embarked on a fundamental process of reform and modernization that has resulted in an unprecedented rate of economic development.[1] If present trends continue unabated, China may be able to present a serious geopolitical challenge to the United States.

This study was undertaken to examine the effects of China's economic development and its efforts at defense modernization. Chapter Two deals with the determinants of Chinese behavior in the short and long terms and the political-military challenges that China might pose. However, the distinction between the short and long terms is not made in terms of a given time frame; rather the earlier period is that during which Chinese policy is primarily concerned with "catching up" with the advanced industrial world, while the latter refers to a possible future period in which China accords priority to other goals, either because it assesses that it has achieved the status of an "advanced" nation in economic, technological and military terms, or for some other reason.

Chapter Three examines Chinese military developments, concentrating on the modernization program by means of which China hopes to transition from its current force to a more modern one.

---

[1]One of the most "optimistic" recent estimates sees China's gross national product (GNP) (as measured in terms of purchasing power parity) surpassing that of the United States in 2006. (China "stable growth" case in Wolf et al., 1995, p. 9.) It should be noted that this estimate was made well before the onset of the current Asian financial crisis; it is, however, unclear whether the crisis, whatever its short-term effects, will have a major effect on such long-range estimates.

The concluding section, Chapter Four, discusses what these developments mean for the United States, both in terms of its overall policy toward China and of the specifically military implications for the U.S. Air Force.

Chapter Two

DETERMINANTS OF CHINESE NATIONAL SECURITY BEHAVIOR

In examining the determinants of Chinese national security behavior, we look first at what appear to be the primary drivers of Chinese policy, from the perspective of the current leadership in Beijing.[1] Because this perspective appears to be dominated by an overriding objective of modernizing the country, the natural division between the short and long runs (assuming the continuation of the current mind-set) is the future time at which China, in the judgment of its leadership, will have achieved a degree of development such that "modernization" will cease to be the overriding concern.[2] Of course, this mind-set could change, leading the Chinese leadership to substitute some other priority for modernization, regardless of how "modernized" it regarded the country to be at the time; in that case, we might have to deal with less constrained Chinese national security behavior much sooner.

Obviously, China's achievement of this status will not be a clear-cut event to which one can assign a precise date, even in retrospect; similarly, one cannot say how long the "modernization" should be expected to be the overriding concern. Nevertheless, at some future point, it would seem likely that, if its current policies are successful, the Chinese leadership will no longer believe its main task to be the "modernizing" of the country.

---

[1]This section draws heavily on recent unpublished work by Michael Swaine and Ashley Tellis.

[2]This is admittedly an extremely vague criterion. It is important to emphasize, however, that what is meant is *not* that China will believe that it has "caught up" with the United States in economic, technological, or military terms. Rather, the reference is to the future time when China will cease to define itself as a developing country and will believe instead that it is "in the same league" as the advanced industrial countries.

DETERMINANTS OF POLICY DURING THE "MODERNIZATION" PERIOD

As noted, China embarked on a major program of economic development and reform in 1978. This program has had unprecedented success in increasing Chinese GNP and in creating a large, export-led, private sector. China has also been successful in attracting vast amounts of foreign direct investment, a great deal of it from "overseas" Chinese investors in Taiwan, Hong Kong, and elsewhere. Although the current Asian financial crisis casts some doubt on whether China can continue to grow at such high rates, China's economy remains among the strongest in the region.[3]

Pursuit of "Comprehensive National Power"

This drive for economic development is perhaps the most important determinant of Chinese behavior, both currently and for the foreseeable future. The goal is to make China a developed country, which would have the effect of, among other things, raising the standard of living of the population and preparing the technological-industrial base for a strong military. In Chinese terminology, the goal is to increase the country's "comprehensive national power." This goal has required the leadership of the Chinese Communist Party to make major adjustments in the way in which it has ruled the country and to accept important risks to its ability to sustain its monopoly of power. In pursuit of modernization, the leadership has greatly relaxed its internal controls over the population and has opened the country to foreign influences.

Thus, the growth of the private sector[4] automatically reduces the leadership's control of the economy, which is governed more by

---

[3]China also faces serious economic challenges with respect to its state-owned enterprises (SOEs), many of which have been losing increasing amounts of money as competition from the private sector and imports has increased, and with respect to its banking sector, which is burdened with large, nonperforming loans made to keep many of these same SOEs afloat. The key question for the immediate future is whether the private sector can grow fast enough to absorb the workers who will inevitably be laid off in the course of restructuring the SOEs and reforming the banks.

[4]It is true that much of what might appear to be the "private sector" involves government officials or members of their families in one way or another, either as owners or as extralegal beneficiaries. In addition, much of the economic development that has occurred outside the (centralized) "state" sector is controlled by local governments at

market forces: This is true to some extent even in such politically charged areas of the economy as publishing. Politically, the change is even greater: The state is no longer the sole employer, and an increasing part of the labor force is no longer monitored and controlled by the system of "work units." Similarly, the expansion of exports and foreign direct investment implies that ordinary Chinese will have much greater contact with the outside world than previously; the pursuit of technological development has also meant that tens of thousands of young Chinese travel abroad every year to enroll in foreign universities. While the leadership may wish them only to absorb the foreigners' science and technology, the students cannot help but be affected by their hosts' political ideas as well. In addition, the modernization drive implies a much greater availability of telecommunications technology, including not only telephones and faxes but also computers and Internet connections.[5]

The primacy of the development objective has also placed some restraints on the regime's foreign-policy actions. The leadership has recognized that good relations with the United States are strongly advisable, if not absolutely necessary, for the success of this program, given Washington's technological leadership and political influence with the other advanced industrial nations. In general, China seeks to take advantage of its relatively good security situation (i.e., the absence of a perceived major threat to the country) to concentrate on increasing its "comprehensive national power" while building up its military capabilities at a moderate pace.

While this basic thrust would seem to require a policy of accommodation with respect to the United States, there are limitations and countervailing forces. Two other determinants of Chinese policy—sovereignty concerns and regime maintenance—limit the extent to which maintaining good relations with the United States can be a governing objective of Chinese policy.

---

the township and village levels. Nevertheless, even enterprises of this sort represent a certain threat to central state power, either because they operate according to market incentives or because they provide local officials with a "private" interest that may conflict with the directives coming from Beijing.

[5]For example, it appears that, within China, the Internet was a primary source of news concerning the anti-Chinese riots in Indonesia in the summer of 1998; the dissemination of this news led to some public protest activity in China, to which the government finally responded.

Sovereignty Concerns

In diplomatic parlance, China is an "unsatisfied power"—a country that claims rightful possession of territories it does not in fact control, the most important of which is Taiwan. In 1972, China agreed essentially to shelve the Taiwan issue, seemingly indefinitely, in the interests of forming a quasialliance with the United States against the more-threatening Soviet Union.[6]

In the late 1980s, however, the ground shifted somewhat: In 1972, the U.S. "acknowledgment" that Chinese on both sides of the Taiwan Strait agreed that there was only one China was generally accurate, at least with respect to the ruling circles on both sides of the Taiwan Strait. However, it became less so as the leadership of Taiwan's ruling party, the Kuomintang, passed into the hands of native Taiwanese, rather than mainlanders who had fled the Communist takeover in 1949. Thus, China faced the possibility that indefinite delay in recovering Taiwan could lead to a consolidation of the island's *de facto* independence in ways that would make eventual unification more difficult, if not impossible.

China's response to this situation has been bifurcated: On the one hand, China has sought to entice Taiwan by offering seemingly favorable terms for reunification (under the rubric of "one country, two systems"[7]); on the other hand, it has engaged in saber rattling to warn Taiwan against pursuing an enhanced international standing. Thus, in March 1996, in connection with the first democratic presidential election in Taiwan, the Chinese mounted provocative military exercises, which included the firing of missiles to areas just off Taiwan's two major harbors, to express their displeasure with President Lee Teng-hui's campaign for international recognition and, presumably, to harm his reelection campaign.[8] Lee had been

---

[6]In return, China received the U.S. "acknowledgment" that Chinese on both sides of the Taiwan Strait believed in the existence of one China.

[7]A formula initially proposed by Deng Xiaoping in the late 1970s, when the People's Republic of China (PRC) may have believed that the U.S. de-recognition of the Republic of China offered a favorable opportunity for reunification.

[8]In the event, Lee Teng-hui won reelection with an absolute majority, indicating that the Chinese effort may have backfired (by inducing independence-minded voters, who might otherwise have supported the opposition Democratic Progressive Party [DPP], to vote for Lee).

conducting a vigorous diplomatic campaign to win recognition for Taiwan in various international organizations, most notably the United Nations. In addition, Beijing saw his "unofficial" trip to the United States in 1995 in connection with an alumni event at his alma mater, Cornell University, as a provocative step. Despite the risk of a confrontation with the United States (the chances of which Chinese leaders may have underestimated, but which occurred when the United States sent two carrier battle groups to the region[9]), China evidently felt it necessary to take strong measures to discourage continued efforts by Taiwan toward securing international recognition.

Similarly, China has been willing to use military force to assert its claims in the South China Sea despite the possibility that such actions could disrupt relations with the other claimant states. Until 1995, many believed that China would use force only against Vietnam, as it had done in 1974 (when it seized some islands in the Paracels group from South Vietnam) and 1988, since Vietnam's own relations with its Southeast Asian neighbors were not particularly close. Once Vietnam joined the Association of Southeast Asian Nations (ASEAN), China could no longer assume that the other states in the region would look on such action with equanimity. However, in February of 1995, China stationed armed vessels at, and built permanent structures on, an islet (Mischief Reef) claimed by, and relatively close to, the Philippines. In general, however, China has attempted to defer questions of sovereignty with respect to the South China Sea while promoting the idea of bilateral "joint development" of the region's resources. Such a stance both preserves China's claims and delays any decisive confrontation, presumably until such time as China is in a better position to vindicate its claims against its rivals.

Despite this relative moderation in terms of policy (at least as compared to past nationalisms of other rising powers, such as Germany from the 1860s to World War II), some observers have noted a rising

---

[9]According to John W. Garver,

> The proponents of military action against Taiwan pointed to the fact that during the high-level Sino-U.S. interactions during 1995, the U.S. side gave only weak and ambiguous warnings against Chinese use of military force against Taiwan.... It seemed that any action short of outright war would be tolerated by Washington. (Garver, 1997, p. 112.)

tide of nationalist sentiment in Chinese officialdom, particularly in the People's Liberation Army (PLA), as well as among some segments of the public.[10] This sentiment is no doubt fueled by China's economic dynamism and its (so far, at least) successful reincorporation of Hong Kong. The sense that China has finally found the right formula for modernizing itself and that it is not condemned to weakness, backwardness, and national humiliation has fed the idea that China can indeed become a great power. Whether, and how, this sentiment will affect foreign policy remains unclear.[11]

Regime Maintenance

The economic reform program embarked on in 1978 essentially replaced communist ideology by pragmatism: In Deng Xiaoping's phrase, "It doesn't matter whether the cat is black or white, as long as it catches mice." Nonetheless, the communist-style political structure remained, as did the principle of one-party rule. In the long run, this necessarily raises the question of the basis of the regime's legitimacy and its ability to maintain power.

This issue is addressed by the two sources of behavior discussed above. To the extent that the regime is successful in promoting China's comprehensive national power and is able to gratify nationalist aspirations, it may expect that its legitimacy will be enhanced. So far, the country's economic success has been remarkable and has been a positive factor with respect to legitimacy; whether China will suffer from the current Asian financial crisis in any major way remains to be seen.

---

[10]In a review of a Chinese book that claimed that China would "become the leading power in the world by the third decade of the next century," John W. Garver notes that "[t]his book is representative of recent nationalist tracts designed to fan and profit from patriotic ardour in contemporary China" and that "[t]here is a profitable market in China today for books that contain forceful and proud patriotic rhetoric—they are popular with the reading public . . . ." Garver goes on to express his "hunch" that the book "does reflect the thinking of at least some Chinese officials." Interestingly, the book was banned shortly after it appeared. (Garver, 1998, pp. 61, 66.)

[11]Wang Jisi, director and senior researcher at the Institute of American Studies of the Chinese Academy of Social Sciences, has argued that, while "nationalist emotions" have blackened the image of the United States in China, Chinese foreign policy is not substantially affected by them, since "Beijing's attitude toward the United States . . . has its origins in China's domestic goals and needs . . . ." (Wang, 1997, p. 14.)

The recovery in July 1997 of Hong Kong, the loss of which to Britain had marked the beginning of China's modern period of national "humiliation," no doubt burnished the regime's nationalist credentials and strengthened its legitimacy. On the other hand, nationalist passions that the leadership is unable to satisfy fully may prove dangerous for regime maintenance, and the leadership has often sought to damp down any expression of them. Recent cases in which the regime has been notably reluctant to pursue a nationalist cause that found resonance with politicized segments of the population include the fracas resulting from actions by Japanese rightists to assert, in a publicity-seeking manner, Japan's claims to the Senkaku/Daioyutai islands (in 1996 and 1997) and the response to riots, largely directed against ethnic Chinese, in Indonesia in the summer of 1998. Thus, while the regime has played the nationalist card when convenient, it does not appear that the usefulness of nationalism as a legitimating principle has induced the leadership to engage in foreign adventures that it would otherwise have chosen to avoid.

When it comes to what are seen as serious threats to the regime, of course, the goal of regime maintenance takes precedence. As the armed response to the student protests in Tiananmen Square in Beijing in spring 1989 showed, considerations of foreign opinion (even when they may lead to actions that hinder China's economic growth, such as economic sanctions, decreased investment, etc.) will take second place under such circumstances.

On the other hand, as noted, the opening up to the rest of the world inherent in the pursuit of comprehensive national power poses a continuing, if low-level, threat to the long-term viability of the regime. While some efforts can be made to hinder the free flow of information from the rest of the world into China, the type of isolation from outside influences typical of past Communist regimes cannot be maintained if China is to derive substantial economic and technological benefit from foreign trade and investment. Thus, while there is likely to be episodic concern about "spiritual pollution" and "peaceful evolution,"[12] it seems unlikely that a significant turn toward a policy of cutting China off from the rest of the world could occur.

---

[12]"Peaceful evolution" is the Chinese term for the supposed U.S. policy of subverting Communist rule in China by means of long-term cultural influences.

Dissatisfaction with the Current International System

China appears to view the current international system, in which the United States, as the only "superpower," often seeks to act in a "hegemonic" manner, as inherently unsatisfactory. While this feeling is probably less important for determining policy than the ones discussed above, it often finds some expression in Chinese diplomatic activity.

At the beginning of the 1990s, many Chinese observers, in agreement with many Western analysts of the international scene, predicted that the predominance of the United States would erode, and a "multipolar" international system would come into existence. This was based in part on the notion that Japan and Germany, in particular, were outperforming the United States economically, while the United States was "overextended" by virtue of its higher defense burden and its role in the world. Eventually, however, this belief in the fragility of the U.S. position was refuted by events, and Chinese analysts tended to see the shift to multipolarity as a longer-term proposition.

In any case, replacing the current international system with a multipolar one in which China will be one of several relatively equal "great powers" is an ostensible objective of Chinese policy. However, it is unclear how important it really is as an actual driver of behavior. In 1996–1997, when Sino-U.S. relations were strained, the Chinese succeeded in incorporating statements in favor of "multipolarity" into the communiqués of President Jiang Zemin's summit meetings with presidents Boris Yeltsin of Russia and Jacques Chirac of France.[13] More generally, China appeared to be following a policy of developing its contacts with Western European nations to broaden its options for economic and technological relationships. Western European countries could in principle become sources of foreign investment and technological know-how; it is hard, however, to imagine them substituting for the United States as a market for Chinese exports.

---

[13]"Joint Statement by the People's Republic of China and the Russian Federation on the Multipolarization of the World and the Establishment of a New International Order" (1997) and "'Text' of Beijing-Paris Declaration" (1997).

However, China enthusiastically took advantage of the opportunity to improve relations with the United States in connection with the Jiang-Clinton summits of October 1997 and June 1998; indeed, instead of welcoming the failure of U.S. nonproliferation policy represented by the nuclear tests that India and Pakistan conducted in spring 1998, China joined with the United States in issuing a statement opposing them.[14] Thus, one could argue that, for the present at least, the Chinese play the multipolarity card only when relations with the United States are strained; otherwise, improving Sino-U.S. relations takes precedence over weakening U.S. "hegemony."

There might be good reasons, despite their occasional rhetoric, the Chinese do not actually seek a multipolar world. One could question whether true multipolarity would be advantageous to the Chinese, given their proximity to three potentially strong "poles" with whom they have had conflictual relations in the past: Russia, Japan, and India. A strong United States that could help keep these countries from becoming threats to China might be a preferable situation. Thus, while opposing U.S. "hegemony," the Chinese might in fact prefer to replace it by something resembling a Sino-U.S. "condominium" rather than multipolarity,[15] either with respect to East Asia, or eventually even on a global basis. This is, however, entirely speculative; any type of "condominium" would contradict standard Chinese rhetoric about the evils of hegemony and "power politics."[16]

---

[14]This is hardly surprising, given that India had justified its nuclear tests in anti-Chinese terms. Nevertheless, the Chinese attitude contrasts strikingly with the earlier Maoist view of nuclear nonproliferation as a kind of conspiracy of the developed "haves" against Third World "have-nots," and this attitude represents a corresponding willingness to support what in other contexts would appear as "hegemonic" behavior on the part of the United States. It betokened less an interest in hegemony-destroying multipolarity than an eagerness to sign up as a junior partner in exercising that hegemony in South Asia. ("Joint Statement by Chinese and US Heads of State on the South Asian Issue," 1998).

[15]In this context, it might be recalled that the Chinese at times interpreted détente and strategic arms control as elements of a joint Soviet-U.S. policy of shared global predominance.

[16]Shambaugh (1997) discusses the possibility of a close alignment of China and the United States that would amount to a "condominium of power over Asia" but judges it as unlikely on the grounds that an "increasing clash of values and interests [between Beijing and Washington is] inevitable as China grows stronger and more hostile to the United States." (Shambaugh, 1997, p. 22.)

Other Factors that Could Affect Chinese Behavior

The perspective of the current Chinese leadership could be affected or modified by various factors or developments, or the current leadership could be replaced by a very different one with different views. This section discusses what some of the modifications could be and how Chinese foreign-policy behavior might change under the circumstances.

"Acculturation" to the International Order. One optimistic view relies on an "acculturation" process, by which the Chinese leadership becomes more and more willing to abide by the general norms of the current international system. Thus, this theory goes, although China's current acquiescence in these norms may be tentative and "insincere," driven solely by the need for foreign contributions to China's modernization, the leadership will gradually come to understand that these norms can serve China's interests as well. By the time China becomes strong enough to challenge the current international order, it will have become reconciled to it.

For example, this view might argue, while China's earlier commitments not to export sensitive nuclear-related material to Pakistan may merely have been concessions to the United States, India's nuclear tests may have convinced China that a global nonproliferation norm is actually in its interest. Similarly, as China develops economically, it may see a global free-trade regime as useful and beneficial to itself[17] and may embrace the World Trade Organization (WTO) whole-heartedly, as opposed to its current attempts to join the WTO while still being allowed to protect its SOEs from foreign competition.

While a view of this sort is sometimes implied in arguments in support of a policy of engagement, it is hard to judge its validity. To some extent, it derives support from the idea (see below) that those governing a modern state have no choice but to adapt to the global international order. However, just because one recognizes that traffic laws are necessary to prevent chaos does not mean that one might not be tempted to run a red light on occasion; whether "accult-

---

[17]For example, by forcing its own companies to perform at world-class standards.

uration" can be expected to extinguish that behavior is a difficult question.[18]

Democratization. The opening of China to the world; the relaxation of restrictions on travel and communications; and the rapid growth of an educated middle class, a large part of which works in the private sector, also raise the possibility of a transformation of the Communist Chinese regime in the direction of more democracy. Of course, this is by no means a foregone conclusion. Even in its "liberal" phases, the Chinese leadership has been willing to take only small steps in this direction; it is ever mindful of the risk that liberalization can go much farther than its initiators intend or can handle.

The importance of this development for foreign policy depends on the validity of the concept of "democratic peace," according to which democratic states do not fight wars with one another for structural and normative reasons. Thus, if China democratizes, the competitive character of its current antagonisms vis-à-vis Taiwan, Japan, Southeast Asia, the United States, and India largely disappears; consequently, China could be expected to follow a generally cooperative strategy similar to that followed by all other states in the so-called "zone of peace" (e.g., the North Atlantic Treaty Organization and Japan).

The notion of democratic peace has engendered serious debate, which cannot be entered into here. While it may well be true that a democratic state that is devoted primarily to increasing the welfare of its citizens is likely to wish to cooperate in the current international order, there are at least two important caveats to be kept in mind.

The first has to do with the difficulties associated with the transition to democracy. Once China becomes completely democratic, the question of adversarial relations between itself and its neighbors may well disappear, but until that point is reached, the issue of how changes in the current regime affect the propensity for conflict and cooperation remains both real and relevant. According to one recent contribution to the debate,

---

[18]Despite his support for a policy of engagement, Shambaugh (1996), p. 209, concludes that "[t]he insular and defensive character of Chinese politics and nationalism suggests that China will be reluctant and difficult to engage and to integrate into the existing international order."

countries do not become democracies overnight. More typically, they go through a rocky transitional period, where democratic control over foreign policy is partial, where mass politics mixes in a volatile way with authoritarian elite politics, and where democratization suffers reversals. In this transitional phase of democratization, countries may become more aggressive and war-prone, not less, and they do fight wars with democratic states. (Mansfield and Snyder, 1995, p. 5.)

Second, the notion of democratic peace relies on the notion that the pursuit of economic self-interest will dominate over other passions in the bulk of the population. Thus, a procedurally democratic state whose population is in the grip of religious fanaticism should not be expected to be particularly peaceful. Similar, a population infected by virulent nationalism could—quite democratically—support war-like policies. While China's modernization can be expected to increase the weight of those who wish to follow pragmatic policies of economic development, it may also prove to be an incubator for nationalist passions. Indeed, in recent incidents (the fracas caused by Japanese rightists' action on the Senkaku/Daioyu islands and the anti-Chinese riots in Indonesia), the leadership appeared to fear that popular nationalist passions could get out of hand and has sought, generally speaking, to dampen them.

Weakness or Collapse. Finally, China could face some sort of chaos or collapse. A crisis of this sort could have various causes spanning the economic, social, and political realms. Economic progress in China has been uneven: The rising regional disparities between the coastal and inland provinces, coupled with the increasingly pervasive corruption seen at all levels in Chinese society, are viewed as preparing the way for consequential challenges to regime legitimacy and even civil war.[19] Even if such outcomes can be avoided, some argue that China's successes cannot be sustained: The continuing growth in the absolute size of the population; the peculiarity of its demographic composition, including the large youthful population combined with a dramatic shortage of females (caused by selective abortion and infanticide); and the problems of shifting a high proportion of the rural population into the urban sector are seen as

---

[19]See the series "Fragile China," *Far Eastern Economic Review*, May 11, 1995, for a good overview of some of these problems.

making for substantial social chaos, not to mention consequential economic interruptions (Mulvenon, 1997).

In addition, China may face severe environmental problems: A significant shortage of potable water is forecast because the water table appears to be falling at the rate of almost 1 m per year in the northern parts of China, and massive environmental degradation is assessed as affecting agricultural output and public health, perhaps even leading to international disputes. (Cohen, 1995.)

The political challenges are also perceived to be both daunting and unmanageable. Despite the clear success of the Chinese economy in the past 20 years, pessimists note that the central government has been increasingly unable to siphon off the growing wealth proportionately through taxation, thereby resulting in the new elites being progressively able to undercut the regime's own power and preferences (Shirk, 1993). This problem, caused by the rise of new power centers in China with all the threats they embody for cohesion and unity, is exacerbated by fundamental disputes within the ruling regime itself. These disputes center on the degree of control that ought to be maintained over the economy, polity and society, the pace of change, and the appropriate methods of change (Kaye, 1995). The future of the PLA, its relationship to the party, and the dilemmas afflicting its principal missions—defense of the country against external threats and defense of the party against internal opposition—all make the looming crisis of governability even more treacherous and burdensome.[20] Finally, the decline in the party's direct control over society; the increasing discontent within its traditional bastions of support, the peasants and workers; and the rise of a new generation of successful social elites who care little for the party or the traditional Communist regime are together seen as producing a situation in which Communist Party control of the country could be seriously threatened.

While these eventualities may be unlikely, it would be hard to argue that they are not possible. What they mean for Chinese foreign-policy behavior or for China's impact on the international system is much harder to say. It is possible that a failing regime would be

---

[20]For an excellent analysis of China's current civil-military dynamic, see Joffe (1996). See also Paltiel (1995).

tempted to undertake a nationalist crusade (such as the immediate incorporation of Taiwan into the PRC) as a means of rallying popular support. Conversely, a weak regime might, for example, be unable to withstand popular nationalist sentiment to do something about mistreatment of ethnic Chinese in a Southeast Asian country. Alternatively, a weak regime might become more inward-looking and be less focused on, and/or less capable of, vindicating its claims to Taiwan or the South China Sea. In any case, a chaotic China could become a source of refugee flows that could threaten to swamp neighboring countries or that could encourage non-Han populations in China (such as the Uighurs in Xinjiang) to pressure Beijing for more autonomy or even independence.

DETERMINANTS OF POLICY IN THE "POSTMODERNIZATION" PERIOD

In the preceding discussion, Chinese foreign-policy behavior was considered in a short-term context; without trying to be precise with respect to the time frame, the essential point was that the period in question was that during which the pursuit of comprehensive national power would continue to be the predominant consideration. But this obviously poses the question of what might determine Chinese behavior once the development process has proceeded to the point that modernization is no longer the overriding concern of the Chinese leadership. As noted above, this does not imply that China will have equaled the United States in either technological level or GNP per capita any time in the foreseeable future, or ever. However, during the Cold War the Soviet Union was not an equal of the United States in either sense; furthermore, it never came close to equaling the United States in terms of GNP, a feat the Chinese may accomplish in the first decades of the next century. Thus, the modernization program launched by Deng Xiaoping sought, if not to allow China to "catch up" with the most economically and technologically advanced nations of the world, at least to promote it to the same league; but what happens if that program succeeds?

Obviously, any attempt to discuss how Chinese foreign-policy behavior might be affected by circumstances that are at least several decades away will be speculative and fraught with uncertainty. With that caveat, one can make use of several theoretical approaches that suggest how Chinese behavior might evolve.

Realist Theory

The long tradition of realist international theory suggests that a "modernized" China with a GNP equal to or greater than that of the United States (and hence with roughly comparable military potential) would inevitably become a major rival for world power.[21] According to one theorist, a rising power like China would challenge the predominant power (the United States) because of the

> increasing disjuncture between the existing governance of the system and the redistribution of power in the system. Although the hierarchy of prestige, the distribution of territory, the rules of the system, and the international distribution of labor continue to favor the traditional dominant power or powers, the power base on which the governance of the system ultimately rests has eroded because of differential growth and development among states. This disjuncture among components of the international system creates challenges for the dominant states and opportunities for the rising states in the system. (Gilpin, 1981, p. 186.)

According to this theoretical outlook, a China that approached or equaled the United States in power would seek to vindicate its territorial claims, attain regional hegemony, increase its status in global terms, and alter the rules of the international system to its advantage.

Vindication of Territorial Claims. At present, China has typically been willing to shelve its territorial claims (while not abandoning them in principle). While there have been some exceptions to this (for example, Chinese occupation of the Paracel islands in 1974, of Johnson Reef and neighboring islets in the Spratlys in 1988, and of Mischief Reef in 1995), China has not, in general, pressed its territo-

---

[21]Even if China had a GNP equal to that of the United States, its larger population (and hence lower GNP per capita) would presumably imply that a smaller percentage of that GNP could be devoted to defense in case of an all-out mobilization effort. (On the other hand, even in case of an all-out mobilization on the model of World War II, the U.S. standard of living would probably remain well above that of China.) However, the more relevant measure might be the resources that could be devoted to defense under conditions short of all-out war (such as those that obtained during the Cold War); under such circumstances, China would be able to match U.S. defense spending without great difficulty. The relative technological level, however, would still favor the United States. Nevertheless, as the Soviet Union showed, a willingness to focus technological and economic resources on military industry can, to some extent, make up for a less-capable industrial base.

rial claims militarily, even when it was relatively well positioned to do so.[22] Even with respect to the most important of these territorial claims, Taiwan, the Chinese saber rattling of 1995 and 1996 was not so much a challenge to the *status quo* as a response to Taiwanese moves to increase its international maneuvering room.[23]

However, there is no reason to believe that such restraint would still prevail were China to achieve "great power" status equal to that of the United States. While there may be some territorial claims on the books about which China is really indifferent (for example, northeastern India), China could, in most cases, expect that its regional military predominance would enable it to settle these disputes on favorable terms, except perhaps when the regional adversary had backing from a "great power" (e.g., Taiwan, assuming it retained U.S. support). To what extent other powers (such as the United States, in the case of Taiwan or the Senkaku/Daioyu islands, claimed by both China and Japan) would be willing to take on China "in its own backyard" is unclear.

Regional Hegemony. Beyond the specific territorial claims, China might expect to exert a predominant influence in its own region, i.e., to attain "regional hegemony" or a "sphere of influence" in traditional diplomatic parlance. This would reveal itself in the deference paid to China by its neighbors, i.e., their willingness to accommodate Chinese interests and preferences with respect to major foreign-policy actions. This could result in limitations on U.S. military, political, and economic access to the region, as China seeks to assert its primacy.

For example, China could become more hostile to the forward basing of U.S. forces in East Asia and U.S. naval deployments to the Western

---

[22]Most notably, China unilaterally withdrew from claimed territories in northeastern India it had occupied in the course of its border war with India in 1962. The Chinese attack on a Soviet border patrol in March 1969 (which took place on a disputed island in the Ussuri River) seemed to be less an attempt to take the disputed territory by force than to sharpen the conflict with the Soviet Union for reasons related both to domestic politics and to the competition between the Chinese and Soviet Communist Parties for influence over other communist parties in Asia. On this latter point, see Ch. 3 of Wich (1980).

[23]Even the earlier Taiwan Strait crises of 1954–1955 and 1958 were more complicated in motivation than merely attempts to take possession of either the offshore islands or Taiwan itself.

Pacific.[24] If Korea were to unify, China could seek to influence or pressure it to close all U.S. military facilities on the peninsula.

Similarly, China could try to increase its economic influence in the region by supporting regional opposition to U.S. economic initiatives, such as attempts to open markets. While the states of the region have some common complaints about U.S. trade and other economic pressures (e.g., protection of intellectual property rights), the United States is likely to remain an important market for regional states, limiting China's ability to unify them on an anti-American platform.

Enhanced Global Status. Realist theory suggests that a rising China will seek to enhance its status on a global scale, both as a matter of prestige and to play a larger role in the settlement of major issues on a worldwide basis. This would involve inherent conflict with the United States, which now enjoys unprecedented global influence. How exactly this would play itself out, however, is difficult to foresee and will depend on which extraregional issues China considers most important.

Changing the Rules. Realist theorists, such as Gilpin, typically see one of the major benefits of high global status as being the ability to affect the international "rules of the game." Thus, the liberal free-trade regime (as incorporated, for example, in such international regimes as the General Agreement on Tariffs and Trade and the WTO) reflects, in this view, the preferences of the United States, which currently enjoys predominant global status. The same may be said of the extent to which respect for human rights has become a quasi-norm of international life, especially as reflected in such documents as the United Nations Declaration of Human Rights and the International Covenant on Civil and Political Rights.[25]

Presumably, a strong China that had obtained equal global status with the United States would set about changing some of these "rules of the road" to better reflect its own interests and preferences. What

---

[24]While China has generally opposed U.S. bases in the region as a matter of principle, it has not made a big issue of them.

[25]Calling respect for human rights a quasi-norm does not, of course, mean that nations necessarily abide by it or even intend to. But however weak the international "norm" may look from an American perspective, it is obviously too strong for the Chinese and many others, who resent it as interference in their internal affairs.

this means in practice, however, is far from clear. At present, China strongly promotes the notion of "noninterference" in internal affairs as a way to ward off American pressures for democracy and human rights. But it is unclear whether China would hold to this position once it became stronger and was in a position to shape international norms.[26]

Chinese Historical Record

The predictions of realist theory are generally consonant with an analysis of Chinese historical behavior, although it is important to recognize at the outset that the international situation of the PRC differs greatly from the one its imperial predecessors faced. Instead of being surrounded by nomadic populations or ethnic groups that looked to China as a cultural model, modern China has as its neighbors nations that may be as advanced as China in economic and technological terms and that enjoy strong and stable national identities. Furthermore, instead of being the largest power in a relatively closed East Asian system, China is now but one power, albeit a potentially great one, in a global system containing several major powers and one superpower. Thus, one must be careful in trying to extrapolate from China's traditional behavior to how it might act in the present or future. With that caveat in mind, however, we can look at China's traditional behavior for some clues.

---

[26]China has recently deviated from a stance of strict noninterference in the interests of overseas Chinese. In the wake of anti-Chinese rioting in Indonesia, the official Chinese Communist Party newspaper, *Renmin Ribao* [People's Daily], reported that

> the Chinese government has made several representations with the Indonesian government through diplomatic channels, expressing its strong concerns and worries over the unjust treatment of the Chinese and overseas Chinese in the country. It has demanded that the Indonesian government investigate the incidents thoroughly, and take effective measures to avoid the occurrence of similar incidents in the future. ("Legitimate Rights and the Interests of the Chinese in Indonesia Must Be Protected," 1998, p. 1.)

This diplomatic activity was presumably made public in response to public protest in China; otherwise, the government might have preferred to keep it secret in deference to its usual noninterference position. (Prior to the Chinese invasion of Vietnam in February 1979, China had strongly protested Vietnamese mistreatment of its ethnic Chinese population; this, however, was neither the real motivation for Chinese hostility nor the formal pretext for the invasion.)

The combination of China's long-standing geopolitical centrality in Asia; high level of economic self-sufficiency; and past economic, cultural, and political influence over the many smaller states, tribes, and kingdoms along its periphery have produced a deep-seated belief in China's political, social, and cultural preeminence in Asia. Within the cosmology of imperial interstate relations, China stood at the top of the pecking order, providing an intellectual and bureaucratic model of proper governance for Chinese and non-Chinese alike. Hence, other states or kingdoms were normally expected to acknowledge the superior position of the Chinese emperor. While this was always the case in theory, Chinese rulers have been highly practical in their approach to statecraft. When confronted with relatively strong potential or actual foes, they have at times adopted far less hierarchical or coercive practices, including the payment of tribute disguised as imperial gifts.

Throughout most of its history, the Chinese state has been more concerned with controlling or neutralizing direct threats to an established geographic heartland originating from a largely fixed but extensive periphery than with acquiring territory or generally expanding Chinese power and influence far beyond China's borders. Historically, the defense of this Chinese heartland required efforts by the Chinese state to control or influence a very large periphery surrounding it, directly or indirectly.[27] During the imperial period, founders of Chinese dynasties often sought to ensure external security by attaining a position of clear dominance over the nearby periphery, preferably through the establishment of unambiguous suzerainty relations backed by superior military force.

For the most of the imperial era (i.e., from the Han Dynasty until the mid-19th century, when the Late Qing Dynasty came into contact with Western imperialist powers), this periphery region primarily encompassed large tracts of land along the northern and northwestern frontiers, i.e., modern-day Xinjiang, Outer and Inner Mongolia, Tibet, and Northeast China (i.e., the former Manchuria). The northern part of present-day Southeast Asia and the Korean Peninsula were only intermittently regarded as a part of China's strategic

---

[27]The central importance of the concepts of core and periphery to Chinese security policy are also stressed by Michael H. Hunt, whose work has influenced this discussion of this complex subject. See, in particular, Hunt (1996).

periphery during the imperial era, whereas ocean regions adjacent to China's eastern and southern coastline, Taiwan, Japan, and the Russian Far East first took on a strategic value only during the Qing Dynasty.[28] Thus, for most of the imperial era, China's strategic periphery consisted primarily of inland regions adjoining its continental borders.

Throughout most of Chinese history, the pacification or control of this periphery was usually regarded as essential to prevent attacks on the heartland and, during various periods of the imperial era, to secure Chinese dominance over significant nearby inland (and, to a much lesser extent, maritime) trade routes. The establishment of Chinese control or influence over the periphery, whether actual (as in the form of military dominance or various types of economic and political arrangements) or largely symbolic (as in the form of tributary relations with periphery "vassal" states and kingdoms), was also considered extremely important during most of the imperial era as a means of affirming the hierarchical, Sinocentric Confucian international order. Even when periphery areas did not pose a significant security threat to the Chinese heartland, or during times of relative Chinese weakness, the symbolic maintenance of a Sinocentric order nonetheless remained an important objective of the Chinese state, to sustain the political legitimacy of the Chinese polity and to deter potential adversaries.

Almost without exception, once imperial rule had been consolidated internally, the early rulers of an imperial Chinese regime would embark on military campaigns in an attempt to absorb adjacent territories into the Chinese heartland, to retake forcibly parts of the heartland lost during the decline of the previous regime, or simply to assert (or reassert) dominant influence over periphery areas by

---

[28]The period of the Southern Song Dynasty constitutes a partial exception to this general statement. At that time, the Chinese state was forced, by the loss of northern China to nomadic powers, to defend increasingly important maritime trade and transport routes along the southern coastline and to ensure the security of China's rivers and tributaries. During the final years of the Song, the growing Mongol threat to China's rivers, lakes, and seacoast prompted a significant expansion of the Song navy. See Swanson (1982), p. 59. For the vast majority of the imperial era, however, inland-oriented Chinese rulers did not view the oceanic regions adjoining China's coastline as a strategic periphery to be controlled through the maintenance of a superior green- or blue-water naval force.

defeating them militarily. For example, the efforts Chinese emperors undertook to reestablish imperial Chinese influence along the periphery were almost exclusively military and often occurred during the initial years of a regime's existence. These campaigns would sometimes extend over many decades (and in some instances persist sporadically for over a century), largely because of the tenacity and high military capabilities of China's opponents.

Most of these military forays were directed against nomadic or semi-nomadic peoples along China's northern and northwestern borders and consisted largely of efforts to ·retake lost territory within the heartland and/or to reestablish Chinese preeminence along the periphery.[29] The use of offensive coercive measures during the early life of an imperial regime was far less prevalent along China's eastern, southern, and southwestern maritime and continental borders. This was largely because most outside powers along those borders were too distant to pose a serious threat to the Chinese heartland (as in the case of Japan[30]), did not possess formidable military forces, or did not repeatedly encroach upon China to acquire the resources needed to maintain or expand their local power position, as did most nearby inner Asian nomadic and seminomadic tribes and kingdoms. Major military actions against China's eastern, southern, or southwestern neighbors during the early life of an imperial regime were usually undertaken as part of an effort to expand Chinese territory or to acquire resources. The most notable example of such behavior consisted of attacks against the ancestors of present-day Vietnamese and other minority tribes residing in present-day southwest China during the Qin, Han, Song, and Ming dynasties.[31] In addition, many early rulers of Chinese imperial

---

[29]Efforts to absorb inner Asian territories into the Chinese heartland were usually unsuccessful and therefore less frequently attempted. The most notable exception to this general pattern occurred during the early Tang, when Turkish troops under the Tang banner extended China's borders deep into central Asia. See Barfield (1989), p. 145.

[30]Japan became a security concern to the imperial Chinese state only during the Ming Dynasty, when Japanese warlord Toyotomi Hideyoshi attacked Korea and tried to conquer China in the 1590s. However, this threat ended with his death in 1598. (See O'Neill, 1987, p. 203.)

[31]The founder of the Qin Dynasty, Qin Shih Huang Di, conquered the Vietnamese state of Nan-Yueh (then occupying parts of present-day southwest China and northern Vietnam) in 214 BC, but the Vietnamese soon regained their independence and

regimes also attempted at various times to absorb parts of present-day Korea.[32]

During the modern era, Chinese contact with industrialized nation-states in the global political arena has injected a strong element of political equality into Chinese perceptions of interstate relations. As a result, since at least the early 20th century, many educated Chinese have stressed the need for China to attain the status, respect, and influence of a major power contending with other major powers in the global arena. Thus, they have stressed the need for China to attain equality with, but not necessarily superiority over, other major powers. However, the notion that China should in some sense enjoy a *preeminent* place among *neighboring Asian states* remains relatively strong among both elites and ordinary Chinese citizens. This is true even though the envisioned form and basis of this preeminence

---

were recognized as a vassal state until 111 BC, when emperor Han Wu Ti retook Vietnam and divided it into nine counties. From 111 BC to 543 AD, Nan-Yueh was the Chinese province of Chiao-chih. It was administered at senior levels by Chinese officials, adopted many Chinese political institutions, and employed Chinese scholars and officials. Strong Vietnamese resistance to Chinese absorption resulted in separation from direct Chinese rule. This eventually led, during the Tang dynasty, to the establishment of Vietnam as a protectorate. With the demise of the Tang, a more independent Vietnamese polity emerged: the Ly Dynasty. Modeled after Chinese imperial regimes, the Ly attempted to establish a position as an entirely separate and equal entity to the Chinese court—the seat of the "southern emperor." Resulting frictions led to a failed effort during the Song to reconquer Vietnam and to the emergence of a tributary relationship as the only alternative to confrontation and war. In the first decade of the 1400s, the early Ming emperor Ming Yongluo reconquered Vietnam (then known as Dai Viet) and attempted to reabsorb it into the Chinese empire as a province under direct Chinese rule. But this effort eventually failed, thus again forcing China to accept a far less intrusive tributary relationship with Vietnam. (See Chen, 1969, pp. 1–9; SarDesai, 1998, pp. 13–35; and Taylor, 1993, pp. 137–150.) As Taylor states (p. 150): "The lesson for the Chinese of their effort to occupy Vietnam was that tributary relations represented a higher wisdom than did a policy of conquest and assimilation."

[32]Han Wu Ti incorporated Korea into the Chinese empire in 108 BC. However, Chinese control was soon limited to the northern part of Korea and was thrown off altogether in 313 AD. The short-lived Sui Dynasty attempted three times to conquer and absorb Korea, without success. The "vigorous warrior kings" of the early Tang had occupied northern Korea by the 660s but were also unable to absorb the kingdom politically. Korea maintained less-intrusive tributary relations with the more-distant Song (which did not occupy most of northern China and hence could not pressure Korea), whereas early Ming and Qing rulers were content to use military, economic, and cultural "persuasion" to establish a more-intrusive form of suzerainty over Korea, which became a virtual protectorate. (O'Neill, 1975, pp. 2, 145, 303–304; Barraclough, 1993, pp. 81, 124; Hucker, 1975, pp. 88–89, 133–134; Fairbank, 1992, p. 114.)

in the modern era may be changing. In particular, the loss of China's cultural preeminence and economic self-sufficiency and the emergence of powerful industrialized nation-states have resulted in a stronger emphasis on the attainment of great power status through economic influence and military might. However, it remains unclear as to whether and to what degree China's aspirations for regional great power status require military dominance over its periphery.

During the modern period, most of the northern and western parts of China's traditional periphery were directly and formally incorporated into China, either by military force and occupation (Tibet and Xinjiang) or by the Sinicization of the region through cultural assimilation and acceptance of Han Chinese migration and settlement (Inner Mongolia and Manchuria). Mongolia itself, however, thanks to its prior status as a client of the Soviet Union, escaped this process. In the east and south, furthermore, China has not established similar control or influence over the surrounding areas: Taiwan has retained its *de facto* independence, and China's claims in the South China Sea have not yet been fully vindicated. Vietnam has been notably undeferential in its attitude toward China; its flouting of Chinese wishes by attempting to become a "regional hegemon" in Indochina led China to "teach Vietnam a lesson" by its short-term invasion of the border area in 1979. Finally, India remains a rival for influence over such buffer states as Nepal and, more generally, in Southeast Asia as a whole; it has tended to have close relations with Vietnam and would be sensitive to any increase in Chinese influence in Myanmar. In addition, India has cultural-religious ties to Tibet, which China has seen as threatening in the past. A strong China might try to address these issues, perhaps using force or the threat of force to help it achieve regional preeminence.

Imperatives of Modernization

While both realist theory and an analysis of Chinese history suggest that a strong China will behave more assertively, especially with respect to its territorial claims and its desire for deference from neighboring countries, a more-optimistic view is also possible. This view derives from the notion that economic and technological strength in the modern world increasingly depends on a nation's ability to benefit from the increasing globalization of the world economy. Even if China's modernization program succeeds in enhancing its comprehensive national power, it would still require good relations with other advanced industrial countries. Thus, even if China's dependence on the outside world were replaced with interdependence, it would still be inhibited in its use of military power, because this could "upset the apple cart" and deny China the benefits of full participation in the world economy.[33]

Similarly, many have argued that the full exploitation of advances in information technology requires nations to adopt a more-open and peaceful attitude toward the rest of the world.[34] In essence, this line of argumentation asserts that, to keep up with technological advances (which have been particularly rapid in areas such as computers and telecommunications), a nation has no choice but to engage heavily in global interchange. This implies not only economic trade but also a willingness to allow relatively unhindered travel and communication. A great deal of contemporary "liberal" international relations theory deals with this issue. In particular, it points to the growing importance of supranational organizations (such as the WTO) and norms of behavior and argues that individual nations will have no choice but to accommodate themselves to this incipient international regime.

The net result, according to this view, is that, unless a nation is willing to fall behind the rest of the world (and start down a path that ultimately leads to North Korean–type poverty), it must surrender a substantial part of its sovereignty to an emerging international order. Thus, a modernized and strong China will find itself confronted with realities that will inhibit tendencies toward assertiveness that would have shown up under earlier historical conditions.

This is not the place to debate the overall validity of this view. However, it is important to note that the argument depends heavily on the *interdependence* of advanced countries in a global economic and

---

[33]The fate of the Soviet Union could (and probably does) serve the Chinese as a negative example in this regard: By the early 1960s, the Soviet Union had, by and large, "caught up" with the West in basic economic and technological terms. Nevertheless, its isolation and autarkic tendencies (combined with the defects of its command economy) meant that it could not keep up, and it soon fell behind with respect to major new technological developments (e.g., in the field of computers).

[34]See, for example, Gompert (1999).

technological system. Thus, while China will be inhibited from taking steps that would hinder the free interchange of goods and information with other countries, other countries will be similarly inhibited when it comes to severing or hindering relations with China.[35] While the danger of "upsetting the apple cart" may inhibit Chinese assertiveness, it will inhibit others' reactions to that assertiveness as well. This might suggest not so much that China would refrain from the use of force to advance its interests but that it would have to use force in a certain way: striking rapidly, to achieve objectives quickly and maximize the psychological shock, so as to present the adversary and its allies with a *fait accompli*. Interdependence implies that the pressure will be on *both* sides to end conflicts quickly and prevent them from escalating to levels that would seriously disrupt trade and other interchange. Whether this will more greatly inhibit Chinese assertiveness or others' reactions to that assertiveness may depend on the cleverness with which each side is able to exploit and manipulate that shared dependence.

WHAT POLITICAL-MILITARY CHALLENGES MIGHT CHINA POSE?

Drawing on the discussion of the current and possible future determinants of Chinese behavior, this section surveys the various political military challenges that China could pose for the United States. The discussion proceeds from the most concrete to the most speculative; its purpose is not to predict future Chinese behavior but to set the stage for considering the implications that Chinese military modernization could have for the U.S. armed forces in general and the USAF in particular.

Vindicating Claims to Territory or Territorial Waters

Like any other state, the PRC can be expected to use force to maintain its territorial integrity. However, unlike most contemporary

---

[35]This phenomenon is already visible in the debates in the United States concerning most favored nation (MFN) trade status for China; despite the fact that China has a large trade surplus with the United States, and is evidently more dependent on Sino-American trade than is the United States, the cost to U.S. business of downgrading relations with China played heavily in the decision making process.

states, the PRC claims, as rightfully belonging to it, territories that it does not currently control.

Taiwan. Of these territories, the most important by far is Taiwan. To vindicate its claim to Taiwan, China explicitly reserves the right to use force.[36] At the same time, it claims to favor the peaceful reunification of Taiwan with the mainland and, indeed, despite past calls for the "liberation of Taiwan," the PRC has not attempted to invade Taiwan or use force directly against it.[37]

During the Cold War, the advantages of a close relationship with the United States were sufficiently important that China was willing to accept an indefinite prolongation of the *status quo*. With the end of a Soviet threat to China, the question arises whether China will be willing to continue to accept this indefinite extension In the context of the return of Hong Kong in 1997, there is at least the possibility that China may prove less patient with respect to this issue.[38]

Beijing's willingness to allow the Taiwanese *status quo* to continue indefinitely presumably depends on whether it believes that time is on its side, i.e., whether it thinks that current trends are pushing Taiwan toward or away from eventual reunification.[39] In either case,

---

[36]During his October 1997 visit to Washington, Chinese President Jiang Zemin asserted (as he had in the past) that this right to use force was "not directed at the compatriots in Taiwan" but only against outside interference. However, he then added to the potential targets of a Chinese use of force "those who are attempting to achieve separation of the country or the independence of Taiwan." ("Clinton and Jiang in Their Own Words," 1997, p. A20.) Presumably, Taiwanese separatists are not "compatriots" even if they live on Taiwan.

[37]In 1954–1955, and again in 1958, the PRC used force against the "offshore islands" (which lie next to the mainland but are controlled by Taiwan), of which the most important are Jinmen (Quemoy) and Mazu (Matsu). It occupied the Dachen group of islands in 1955, but its actions against Jinmen and Mazu have not gone beyond artillery bombardment. Chinese motivations for shelling Jinmen and Mazu were complex. It may have hoped that its 1958 bombardment of the islands, and the consequent difficulty in resupplying them, would lead Taiwan to abandon them, but other motives played a role in China's actions in 1958, as well as in 1954–1955.

[38]For example, then Premier Li Peng stated in a speech on January 30, 1996, that, following the reversion of Macao to Chinese sovereignty in 1999, "[s]ettling the Taiwan issue and completing the great cause of China's reunification will prominently be put before all Chinese people." ("Accomplishing the Great Cause of the Reunification of the Motherland is the Common Wish of All Chinese People," 1996.)

[39]The growth of cross-Strait trade and of Taiwanese investment on the mainland is presumably the major integrative trend. Against that must be set the effects of Taiwan's democratization, the rise to political importance of native Taiwanese (as

Beijing will be sensitive to any steps Taiwan takes toward independence. The PRC's military exercises of early 1996,[40] intended to threaten Taiwan on the occasion of its presidential election, represented a response to what it saw as the provocatively pro-independence policy of Taiwanese president Lee Teng-hui.

Thus, the PRC might be led to use force to incorporate Taiwan into the mainland. This could come in response to some action by Taiwan or others that threatens to make eventual reunification less likely or even impossible (such as a Taiwanese declaration of independence) or at China's own initiative, if it should decide that the underlying political, social, and economic trends are unfavorable to peaceful reunification and are unlikely to be reversed. /

South China Sea and the Spratly Islands. China claims all the islands, reefs, and rocks in the Spratly Islands that are above sea level. (Taiwan, Vietnam, Malaysia, the Philippines, and Brunei also have overlapping claims on all or some of these islands.) In addition, China claims (as does Taiwan) almost the entire South China Sea, including areas that other nations consider parts of their continental shelves.[41] In 1992, China formally asserted these claims in a law that claimed most of the South China Sea as territorial waters and that claimed sovereignty over the Spratly, Paracel, and Daioyutai (Senkaku) islands.[42]

---

opposed to "mainlanders" who came to Taiwan in 1949 and their descendants), and the simple passage of time.

[40]See Garver (1997) for a detailed discussion of these events.

[41]China and Vietnam also dispute the status of the Tonkin Gulf, between northern Vietnam and the Chinese island of Hainan. Vietnam claims that the boundary should be fixed at the longitude specified in the Sino-French border convention of 1887, a line which runs closer to Hainan than to the Vietnamese coast. China, however, regards this agreement as an "unequal" treaty and claims that the boundary should be fixed according to general principles, e.g., along the equidistance line.

[42]"Testing the Waters" (1992), pp. 8–9. Catley and Keliat (1997), p. 83. However, some uncertainty remains about the exact extent of the Chinese claims:

> [B]y its actions, China appears to claim sovereignty over the entire South China Sea, but it refuses to state or justify its claim, aside from publishing maps that show a dashed 'historic claim line' encompassing most of the South China Sea. It is uncertain whether China claims sovereignty to the entire area, above and below sea level, within the historic line or only the islands inside the line. And if it claims the islands only, does it also claim EEZs [exclusive economic zones] and continental shelves from these features, and believe that such zones should extend to the equidistant line with claims from other continents? (Valencia, 1995, p. 13.)

This area is important for several reasons. It is thought to contain significant oil and natural gas deposits, although the estimates of their size have varied widely.[43] In addition, crucial sea routes between the Middle East and East Asia pass through the area; hence, any interference with freedom of navigation would have important economic repercussions.

Each of the claimants, except Brunei, has taken some military action (e.g., occupying an island) to assert its claims. Various clashes have occurred over the years; the most notable took place in 1974 (when the Chinese evicted South Vietnamese forces from some of the Paracel Islands) and in 1988 (when Chinese drove Vietnamese troops away from Johnson Reef in the Spratlys). In 1995, the Chinese established some permanent structures on Mischief Reef, which is also claimed by the Philippines. In the future, China may use force to vindicate its claim to the South China Sea and its islands.

Other Territorial Claims. China claims (as does Taiwan) eight uninhabited islands (known in Chinese as Daioyu, and in Japanese as Senkaku), located about 100 miles north of Taiwan, which are currently controlled by Japan. The area may contain some oil; the islands' location could be strategically significant as part of the "first island chain" that separates China from the open areas of the Pacific Ocean (Sutter, 1992, p. 7).

Over the years, there have been various minor incidents as private citizens of the claimant countries have tried to take actions to assert their respective countries' claims. China acted with restraint in the course of these incidents; one could argue that, above all, it feared stimulating the nationalist passions of its own population. Nevertheless, in the future, were China to feel it advantageous to raise tensions with Japan, it might use force with respect to these islands. While the United States does not take a position with respect to these claims,[44] it could not ignore any Chinese attempt to exert military pressure against its Japanese ally.

---

[43]Valencia (1995), p. 10, gives a range of 1 to 17.7 billion tons (approximately 7 to 125 billion barrels).

[44]The United States controlled these islands after World War II but returned them to *de facto* Japanese control at the time of the reversion of Okinawa (1971). "Since then, the U.S. Government has endeavored to keep from taking sides in the dispute." (Sutter, 1992, p. 7.)

China does not recognize the McMahon Line separating northeast-ern India from Tibet; according to China, the Tibetan officials who agreed to it in 1914 were not authorized to do so. Instead, Chinese maps show the boundary along the foot of the hills, some 50 miles to the south, thereby claiming some 35,000 square miles of territory currently ruled by India as part of the Northeast Frontier Agency. In September 1993, the two countries agreed to "maintain peace and tranquillity" along the existing line of control (Malik, 1995, p. 317). However, they still disagree in principle about the status of the McMahon Line. As of this writing, it is too early to tell whether the Indian nuclear tests of May 1998 will lead to renewed tensions that could cause the border issue to flare up again. The border with Vietnam, disputes concerning which figured prominently in the Chinese justification of its invasion of that country in February 1979, is quiet. However, should Sino-Vietnamese relations deteriorate for some other reason, this issue could be raised to justify Chinese use of force.

To Deal with a Separatist Threat

China faces a series of threats to its territorial integrity from sepa-ratist movements in its non-Han populated region, primarily Tibet, Xinjiang, and Inner Mongolia. For geopolitical or ethnic-religious reasons, support for these separatist movements could come from the region's neighbors, i.e., India, the Central Asian states (primarily Kazakhstan and Kyrgyzstan), and Mongolia, respectively.

In the past, China has accused India of supporting Tibetan resistance to Chinese rule (for example, by providing sanctuary for the Dalai Lama following the 1959 revolt). Perhaps provoked by the Dalai Lama's statement approving the Indian nuclear tests, commentary in the *PLA Daily* has linked the Indian tests to a policy of interference in Chinese internal affairs.[45] However, the Tibetan situation is rela-tively quiescent at the moment.

---

[45]"The five nuclear test explosions have laid bare the lies and schemes of the Indian authorities. China has never invaded India, but India has occupied Chinese territory. India has taken advantage of the Tibetan issue to interfere in China's internal affairs." (Dong, 1998, p. 5.)

Much more serious has been the Uighur opposition in Xinjiang, which has led to a series of violent actions in recent years. China has obtained pledges of "good behavior" from neighboring Central Asian states, which have valued cooperation with China above ethnic or religious solidarity with the Uighurs. (See Burles, 1999.) However, it is worth noting that these states are currently ruled by Soviet-era *apparatchiki* (except for Kyrgyzstan, whose president was a democratically minded dissident during Soviet times). If the future governments of these states take their countries' Muslim and/or national identities more seriously, they may be willing to run some risks vis-à-vis China to help the Uighur resistance.

Finally, there is an ethnic affinity between the Mongolians who live in China (in Inner Mongolia) and those who populate independent Mongolia. In the context of a general loosening of political controls by Beijing, the Mongol population of Inner Mongolia could agitate for greater autonomy, which would raise the question of support from their brethren across the border.

While the Chinese government has blamed "outside influences" for some of the violence in Xinjiang, it has not sought to take action against any of the neighboring states. However, if separatist activity were to become more serious and if neighboring states were to become important bases of support, one could imagine that China would use force to deter the states from supporting separatism and/or to disrupt or destroy separatist bases on their territory.

To Prevent the Emergence of a New Threat to China

With Gorbachev's rise to power in the Soviet Union, the PRC entered a new and unprecedentedly favorable situation; previously, it had always seen a mortal threat to its existence, first from the United States and then from the Soviet Union. While it faced, as it believed, a mortal foreign threat, the PRC held to a doctrine of "People's War": The attacking enemy would be "lured" deep into China, where it would be destroyed piecemeal by opportunistic attacks and guerrilla warfare.[46] This doctrine reflected the fact that the putative threat-

---

[46]Of course, the PRC never implemented this doctrine, for the simple reason that it was never invaded. But it was presumably the doctrine's promise of ultimate victory

ening powers were much stronger than China and that, initially at least, China could do little to prevent them from invading its territory.

Looking forward, however, China must consider whether new threats might not emerge, perhaps from Japan or India. If so, is it conceivable that China might use force to prevent a potential opponent from being able to pose a serious threat? While the United States would be compelled to react to the use of force against its Japanese ally, U.S. involvement in a Sino-Indian dispute would depend on the circumstances at the time.

Present-day Japan presents the anomalous case of an "economic superpower" that is content to be essentially a nonplayer on the world political-military stage. Nevertheless, the Chinese remain intensely suspicious of Japan, not least for historical reasons,[47] and they react strongly to even minor shifts in Japanese policy or practice that might presage a stronger world role. China could be tempted to use force against Japan if it appeared poised to break radically with its recent policies and adopt a more active political-military role.[48] In such a circumstance, China might believe that it could use force to humiliate and discredit forces in Japan that favored a more militarist course and to alarm and energize their opponents, thereby averting the threatened change in Japan's behavior. Alternatively, China might want to secure the disputed islands before Japan became militarily strong enough to contest them.[49] The key point would be not so much what military objective China sought to obtain by its use of force but the expected impact of the incident on internal Japanese opinion and politics. The characteristics of such a use of force—

---

that allowed the PRC to engage in risky actions against stronger opponents, as it in Korea in 1950, the Taiwan Straits in 1954–1955 and 1958, and along the Soviet border in March 1969.

[47]For a discussion of Chinese attitudes toward Japan, see Christensen (1996a), pp. 40–45.

[48]This assumes that the U.S.-Japan alliance had broken down in some fashion, or had for some reason been transformed into an alliance of equals.

[49]Christensen (1996a), p. 44, assesses that, if it appeared that the U.S.-Japan security relationship were foundering, there would be a "widening consensus among Chinese analysts that China should quickly build up its military power and settle various sovereignty disputes in the *East* and South China seas, by force, if necessary." (Emphasis added.)

especially the emphasis on achieving surprise and producing a major psychological shock—would be consistent with past Chinese uses of force.

By contrast, India is an economically; militarily; and, generally speaking, technologically weaker power than China. Nevertheless, India has been an active political-military player in South Asia, and as its nuclear test program makes clear, is intent on increasing its military capabilities to deal with what it sees as a Chinese threat to its security. At least some Chinese observers have questioned whether India has fully acquiesced to the full incorporation of Tibet into China.[50] More generally, in the aftermath of the nuclear tests, Chinese military writers accused India of seeking hegemony in South Asia, as well as "great-power status in the international community." (Zhang, 1998, p. 5.) If this assessment of India's intentions were to become the predominant Chinese one, China might feel compelled to react militarily in case of a future Indo-Pakistani war, especially if it appeared that India was on the verge of a major victory. The border dispute could provide the excuse to act, much as border tensions and incidents provided the pretext for the Chinese invasion of Vietnam in 1979; the real motive had to do with Vietnam's attempt to gain "regional hegemony" by invading Cambodia and installing a friendly government in Phnom Penh.

To Protect Ethnic Chinese Populations or Business Interests

The PRC has not used force to protect ethnic Chinese populations in neighboring countries or its business interests in them. The Chinese complained about the mistreatment of ethnic Chinese in Vietnam in the late 1970s, but the real motive for the Chinese invasion of 1979 must be sought elsewhere: The Chinese remained allied to the Khmer Rouge rulers of Cambodia, who treated Chinese residents of Cambodia far worse than the Vietnamese did. The PRC did nothing to help the thousands of Chinese victims massacred in Indonesia in

---

[50]As noted above, prior to the PRC military occupation of Tibet in 1950, Tibet had, while recognizing formal Chinese "suzerainty," enjoyed varying degrees of autonomy relative to the central government. In addition, Great Britain, when it ruled India, had maintained quasi-diplomatic direct contacts with Tibetan authorities. Upon gaining independence in 1947, India retained the last British representative in Lhasa, Tibet, as its own representative there. (Maxwell, 1970, p. 68.)

1965 (although it should be noted that, given the distance involved, there was probably little it could have done even if it had wished to). Similarly, China has done nothing to help protect the Chinese merchants who were the primary victims of the Indonesian riots caused by the economic crisis of 1997–1998.

One could speculate, however, about whether this might not change in the future. First, the PRC regime will come to depend more heavily on nationalism as a source of its legitimacy the more it departs from communist ideology; this may make it more difficult to ignore the fate of fellow ethnic Chinese in neighboring countries. Second, the process of opening up the Chinese economy has resulted in increased ties between China and the "overseas" Chinese, who have become important sources of investment, trading opportunities, and expertise. As the idea of "Greater China" (the mainland, Hong Kong, Taiwan, and the "overseas" Chinese in Southeast Asia) becomes more important in economic terms, the PRC may have a greater interest in defending the ethnic Chinese of the region. Finally, the Chinese have begun to invest in oil production and transportation facilities in Central Asia, as an important means of satisfying their growing need for energy; this may create a large economic interest in the neighboring countries, which the Chinese may be willing to protect by force if necessary.

To Secure Deference from Regional States

As China becomes economically and militarily stronger, one would expect that it would seek to be treated with a certain degree of deference by its less-powerful neighbors. In particular, China would probably wish to influence the relationship neighboring countries enjoy with powers outside the region, especially the United States, since these relationships could also influence the regional state's behavior in other respects.

One way this could come to a head would be with respect to a regional state's decision to permit U.S. military bases on, or other forms of military access to, its territory. For example, the issue of whether U.S. troops would continue to be based on the Korean peninsula after the country was unified could lead to a crisis and a potential use of force by China. Similarly, U.S. basing in Vietnam might be seen by China as particularly threatening and unacceptable.

To some extent, the Chinese invasion of Vietnam in 1979 could be seen as falling into this category; the Chinese objected to Vietnam's attempt to attain the status of "regional hegemon" in Southeast Asia. However, the context was quite different from what it is likely to be in the future: As a client of the Soviet Union, Vietnam represented a much more serious threat to China (as part of a Soviet "encirclement") than it would in the future.

CONCLUSION

If nothing else, this chapter illustrates the tremendous uncertainties concerning China's future role in the world. Aside from the uncertainties arising from possible domestic political changes (e.g., democratization of the political system and the role of nationalism in legitimating Communist Party rule), one cannot be certain what balance the current leadership will strike between economic development and other "nationalist" concerns, such as reunification with Taiwan, and cannot predict how the leadership will react to the stresses and strains of globalization and an international system that it sees as unduly influenced by the United States. Before discussing what U.S. policy is appropriate in conditions of such uncertainty, we turn to the actual military forces that a future Chinese leadership would be able to bring to bear in support of its interests.

Chapter Three

CHINA'S MILITARY MODERNIZATION

Consistent with its overriding concern for economic development and with its assessment that China does not face a major, direct threat to its territory or regime, the Chinese leadership has not put a great emphasis on its military capabilities, and its defense burden has remained moderate. Nevertheless, revamping the military was one of the "Four Modernizations" promulgated in 1973. It was, however, seen as "a long-term strategic program" as opposed to an urgent requirement, and no dramatic upsurge in the level of Chinese defense spending or effort occurred in the late 1970s and early 1980s (Allen, Krumel, and Pollack, 1995, p. 26). Instead, attention centered on

> redesigning the armed forces . . . so that they would be capable of absorbing and effectively using more advanced weapons and equipment as they became available in the future. (Allen, Krumel, and Pollack, 1995, p. 27.)

The defense research and development (R&D) system and industrial base were likewise to be transformed and more closely integrated into the civilian sector during the first decade of Chinese defense modernization.

By the early 1990s, China's explosive economic growth permitted Beijing to fund steady growth in military spending. As shown in Figure 3.1, the Arms Control and Disarmament Agency's (ACDA) estimate of China's defense expenditures reveals a period of more or less flat budgets followed by an increase in real terms of about 20 percent between 1991 and 1995. Our estimates of Chinese defense

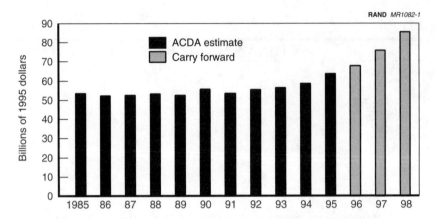

NOTE: For 1985-1995, the ACDA estimates of Chinese defense expenditures, expressed in constant 1995 dollars, are from ACDA (1997), p. 65. For 1996–1998, the real year-over-year increase in Chinese defense expenditures was calculated on the basis of the increase in the official Chinese defense budget (expressed in current RMB), deflated by the implicit gross domestic product (GDP) deflator (which in turn was calculated by comparing the official figures for nominal and real GDP growth). The data for 1996 and 1997 were taken from China Statistical Publishing House (1998), pp. 55, 58, 276. The deflator for 1998 was the increase in consumer prices, as given in Economist Intelligence Unit (1999), p. 6. The official Chinese defense budget for 1998 was taken from IISS (1998), p. 178. The real increases were then applied to the ACDA estimate for 1995 to yield estimates for 1996 through 1998.

Figure 3.1—Estimated Chinese Defense Spending, 1985–1998

spending for 1996 through 1998 suggest a continued acceleration, with the 1998 budget representing a real increase of 54 percent from 1991.[1] While this does not represent a crash program to increase military capabilities at all costs—although Chinese GNP estimates vary widely, the defense burden, by any account, remains relatively light, i.e., below 3 percent—such budget expansion could, if sus-

---

[1]Estimating Beijing's defense spending is a contentious issue among analysts, and the results can vary tremendously depending upon the assumptions used, for example, regarding purchasing-power parity. Some experts put forward considerably smaller figures than the ACDA estimates shown above, while a few propose higher numbers. Various experts, for example, estimate Chinese defense spending at about $20–25 billion less than the ACDA numbers, while Richard Bitzinger argues that the PLA's spending may have reached $143 billion annually in the mid-1990s. (See Bitzinger, 1995, pp. 35–37.)

tained, result in a PLA that is far more up to date and capable than at any time in its history.

The PLA TODAY: "SHORT ARMS AND SLOW FEET"

The Chinese military today is characterized by a set of strengths and weaknesses that set it apart from other defense establishments. Following is a short description of the current PLA, which one senior Chinese officer has described as a boxer with "short arms and slow feet." We then explore some of the ways the Chinese may be trying to extend their reach and increase their dexterity.

Chinese Military—Strategic Strengths

Sizable Forces. China has the largest armed forces in the world; despite a decade of downsizing, which is continuing, the PLA's active strength is roughly 2.8 million compared to, for example, about 1.4 million for the United States and 1.2 million for Russia.[2] China could surely ultimately overwhelm any local adversary by sheer weight of numbers if it could bring anything like the full mass of its forces to bear, but supporting such a large army requires vast resources that could otherwise be used for new weapons or expanded training.[3] Thus, although the PLA derives some strength from its huge size, it does not follow that reducing the size of the PLA will weaken it; if the resources that are freed up by manpower reductions were spent on the procurement of new weapon systems and improving training levels, the net result would likely be an increase in the PLA's overall military capability.

Strategic Nuclear Capability. In addition to its large collection of general-purpose forces, China has an intercontinental nuclear capability. This nuclear threat to the U.S. homeland would certainly loom large in the background of any Sino-U.S. confrontation. The Second Artillery Corps, Beijing's missile force, fields a small number—probably 20—of *Dongfeng* (East Wind) model 5 (DF-5) inter-

---

[2] All estimates from International Institute for Strategic Studies (IISS) (1998).

[3] Many of those demobilized from active service have been transferred to the People's Armed Police, a paramilitary force primarily concerned with maintaining domestic order. Because of that reshuffling, the military drawdown of the last decade has not freed as much modernization funding as it might otherwise have done.

continental ballistic missiles (ICBMs),[4] which can strike targets in most of the continental United States. A new mobile ICBM, the solid-fuel DF-31, is currently being flight-tested, and another advanced ICBM, the DF-41, is reportedly under development.[5]

Since the recent delivery of the Iridium satellites into orbit from Chinese launch vehicles, there has been speculation about the PRC's ability to develop ballistic missiles with multiple independently targetable reentry vehicles (MIRVs). Although much of the technology necessary to place multiple satellites into orbit from a single launch vehicle is applicable to MIRVs, other key technologies are required. First, the placement of reentry vehicles demands a significantly more precise delivery than the orbital transfer maneuver that inserts satellites into an orbit. Second, it is necessary to miniaturize the mass and volume of the nuclear warheads.[6] Third, because of the miniaturization, the MIRV warheads typically have smaller yields and hence must be more accurate. Size constraints may also mean that warheads must be narrower (relative to their length) and hence that they reenter the atmosphere more quickly, in turn requiring advanced materials to shield them against the resulting higher temperatures. Therefore, the successful launch of multiple satellites does not immediately indicate a MIRVing capability but does provide some of the technologies required. According to some observers, the DF-41 is likely to be the first Chinese ICBM to carry MIRVs (Lamson and Bowen, 1996, p. 23).

The other side of the coin regarding MIRV capability is Chinese nuclear weapon doctrine and strategy. It is unclear whether it would be significantly cheaper for the Chinese to MIRV their ICBMs instead of simply building more single–reentry vehicle missiles. Similarly, it is unclear whether there would be, in the absence of arms control restraints, any strategic advantage, either.

---

[4]As with so many questions regarding China's military, there is wide variance in Western estimates of the number of deployed ICBMs. There are reports that six new missiles have been fielded in early 1998 with two more to follow later in the year. (See Gertz, 1998, p. 1.)

[5]The first test launch of the DF-31 was reportedly in May 1995.

[6]Reported Chinese espionage activities directed at gaining access to information about the U.S. W-88 warhead may have been intended to help with this problem.

China has also built at least one *Xia*-class nuclear-powered ballistic-missile submarine (SSBN), but there is some controversy about whether or not she has ever undertaken an operational patrol. China is reportedly developing a follow-on SSBN class (Type 094) that will be deployed after the turn of the century, and the *Ju Lang* (Giant Wave) model 2 (JL-2) submarine-launched ballistic missile (SLBM) is being developed in parallel with its land-based counterpart, the DF-31.

Chemical and Biological Weapons. China ratified the Chemical Weapons Convention in 1997 and claims that it "does not produce or possess chemical weapons."[7] In fact, however, China has

> an advanced chemical warfare program, including research and development, production, and weaponized capabilities. . . . In the near future, China is likely to achieve the necessary expertise and delivery capability to integrate chemical weapons successfully into overall military operations.
>
> China's current inventory of chemical agents includes the full range of traditional agents, and China is conducting research into more advanced agents. It has a wide variety of delivery systems for chemical agents . . . . (Office of the Secretary of Defense, 1997, p. 10.)[8]

China does acknowledge having an "anti–chemical warfare corps" engaged in developing protective technologies and procedures and maintains an anti–chemical warfare "school" and an anti–chemical warfare "institute" (Zhu and Huang, 1997). China is also believed to have transferred chemical weapon precursors and technology to Iran.[9]

China became a party to the 1972 Biological Weapons Convention in 1984, but apparently does not explicitly claim to have eschewed pro-

---

[7]China does admit to having "a significant chemical industry" and claims that it has on its territory "large quantities of chemical weapons abandoned by Japanese aggressor troops" at the end of World War II. (Information Office of the State Council of the People's Republic of China, 1995, p. 18.)

[8]See also Truesdell (1997).

[9]Office of the Secretary of Defense (1997), p. 12; Zabarenko (1993); Meyers (1997); Spector (1996).

duction or possession of biological weapons.[10] Instead, Beijing's official stance is that "China has consistently advocated a complete prohibition and thorough destruction of biological weapons. It opposes the production of biological weapons by any country and their proliferation in any form by any country." (Xinhua News Agency, 1995).[11] In any case, China is believed to have had an offensive biological warfare program prior to its accession to the Biological Weapons Convention in 1984, and this program has likely been maintained. As with China's chemical warfare program, possible delivery systems include ballistic missiles, cruise missiles, and aircraft.[12]

The existence of at least one "antibiological" warfare unit, associated with the Military Medical Research Unit of the Beijing Military Region, is known. The unit apparently conducts research on virulent bacteria, insect carriers of disease, and biological and chemical toxins. It is said to have been established for the purpose of "guarding against and defeating any enemy biological warfare," but presumably its research and technology could be turned to the purpose of creating biological weapons, too, if in fact the unit is not already so engaged. Since this unit is identified as belonging to the Beijing Military Region and its research appears to be focused on China's northern environs, it seems plausible that the other military regions have biological warfare units as well (Yu, Gao, and Gao, 1994, pp. 5–6).

Surface-to-Surface Missiles. The Chinese have also invested heavily to develop a family of short-, medium-, and intermediate-range ballistic missiles (SRBMs, MRBMs, and IRBMs, respectively); these are listed, along with China's ICBMs and SLBMs, in Table 3.1. Many of these missiles can carry nuclear or conventional payloads, and the Chinese are reported to be working on more-advanced warheads for their missiles, including conventional submunitions.

---

[10]ACDA (1996), p. 68.

[11]This difference may reflect the much weaker enforcement mechanisms for the Biological Weapons Convention as compared to the Chemical Weapons Convention or Non-Proliferation Treaty.

[12]ACDA (1996), p. 68; Office of the Secretary of Defense (1997), p. 10; and Truesdell (1997).

Table 3.1

Known Chinese Ballistic Missiles Deployed or Under Development

Name	Type	Development Began	Entered Service	Propulsion	Range (km)	Payload (kg)	CEP (m)	Number Deployed
DF-3	IRBM	~1960	1971	Liquid	2,800	2,150	1,000	~100
DF-4	IRBM	1965	1980	Liquid	5,500	2,200	1,500	20–50
DF-5	ICBM	1965	1981	Liquid	12,000	3,200	500	20
DF-11	SRBM	1984	1992	Solid	280	800	600	200+
DF-15	SRBM	1984	1991	Solid	600	500	300	400+
DF-21	MRBM	~1965	1987	Solid	1,800	600	N/A	30–50
M-7	SRBM	1985	1992	Solid	150	190	N/A	N/A
M-18	IRBM	1984		N/A	1,000+	N/A	N/A	N/A
DF-25	IRBM	N/A		Solid	1,700	2,000	N/A	N/A
DF-31	ICBM	1985		Solid	8,000	700	N/A	N/A
DF-41	ICBM	1986		Solid	12,000	N/A	N/A	N/A
JL-1	SLBM	1967	1983	Solid	1,900	600	N/A	N/A
JL-2	SLBM	N/A		Solid	12,000	700	N/A	N/A

The accuracy of Chinese missiles can be expected to improve, in part because of the integration of global positioning system (GPS) receivers into their inertial guidance systems. GPS assistance alone could reduce the circular error probable for current-generation Chinese missiles by 20 to 25 percent and by up to perhaps 70 percent for future systems (see Frost and Lachow, 1996).[13] The Chinese have also announced plans to deploy their own *Twin Star* satellite navigation system, although its utility for assisting in missile guidance has not, to our knowledge, been assessed.[14]

Geographic Extent. China's large size gives it the defensive advantage of strategic depth. In the past, China has relied on the country's vastness to swallow up an invading army and make it subject to guerrilla-style attack until Chinese forces gained enough strength to expel it. (This view was codified in the doctrine of "people's war.") Under contemporary conditions, China's geographic extent would make it impossible for anyone to subject it to the kind of strategic air campaign to which Iraq was subjected in the 1991 Gulf War—it is difficult to imagine an attacking air force sufficiently powerful to launch crippling simultaneous attacks against the full range of vital military targets throughout the vast Chinese mainland.

Casualty Tolerance. Finally, China has in recent history demonstrated a willingness to absorb substantial casualties in military operations. Precise figures are unknown, but typical estimates for Chinese losses in the 1950–1953 Korean war range from 300,000 to 1 million men. In the 1979 Sino-Vietnamese conflict, Hanoi claims to have killed or wounded 42,000 Chinese in less than a month of fighting, while the Chinese admit to 20,000 casualties (Allen, 1995, p. 92).[15]

---

[13]Chinese engineers have claimed that GPS integration could "raise impact accuracy about one order of magnitude." (Gerardi and Fisher, 1997, p. 129.)

[14]"Chinese 'GPS' Project Set" (1994), p. 25.

[15]Chinese casualties may be compared to the roughly 200,000 U.S. killed and wounded in action in 10 years of combat in Southeast Asia. China's tolerance for large human losses may erode as and if its political system becomes more responsive to the popular will; one could also speculate about the long-term effects of the one-child policy on casualty tolerance.

Chinese Military—Strategic Weaknesses

Obsolete Equipment. Along with these strengths, the PLA suffers from many glaring weaknesses. The Chinese military is mainly equipped with aging, obsolete, and inadequate weapons. The People's Liberation Army Air Force's (PLAAF's) most numerous fighter, for example, is the Shenyang J-6, which is a Chinese-produced copy of the 40-year-old MiG-19 FARMER.[16] The J-6 first flew in 1961, entered service with the PLAAF in 1962, and still constitutes over half of the Chinese air force inventory.[17] Although many older aircraft are being retired, they still account for the lion's share of the PLAAF force structure.

The other services suffer from obsolescence as well, with both the army and navy fielding systems that, for the most part, are based upon decades-old Soviet technology. The army's primary tank is the Type-59, which is a Chinese-produced copy of the Soviet T-54, which entered service in 1953.[18]

The navy likewise boasts an aging fleet of only modest capabilities. Its warships are, with a few exceptions, variants of 1950s-era Soviet designs.[19] They lack long-range air defenses and have serious shortfalls in antisubmarine warfare capability. While the People's Liberation Army Navy (PLAN) has in excess of 40 replenishment vessels, they are—by U.S. standards—small and few, which limits the PLAN's ability to operate at sea for extended periods. (See Yung, 1996, p. 18.)

---

[16]According to IISS (1998), some 1,800 of the PLAAF's 3,000 fighters and bombers are J-6 variants. The MiG-19 entered Soviet service in 1955. (Taylor, 1988, p. 181.)

[17]To put this in perspective, the predominant fighter aircraft in the USAF inventory in 1962—when the J-6 began PLAAF service—was the North American F-100 *Super Sabre*, which last saw squadron service in the active Air Force 25 years ago. The mainstays of the current USAF—the F-15 and F-16—first flew in 1972 and 1974, respectively, when the basic J-6 design was already 20 years old.

[18]According to the IISS (1998), roughly 6,000 of 8,800 main battle tanks in PLA service in 1998 were Type-59s.

[19]For example, the most numerous major surface combatant in the PLAN is the *Jianghu*-class frigate, which is basically "an enlarged variant of the Soviet 'Riga' type." The *Riga* entered fleet service with the Soviet navy in 1955. (Jordan, 1994, p. 276.) For data on the *Riga*, see Polmar (1986), pp. 229–230.

Poor Logistics Support. One example of a more-systemic PLA weakness is that its logistics and supply systems are uncoordinated and wholly inadequate to support any sustained power-projection operations. China has historically lacked the kind of modern transportation infrastructure needed to support large forces engaged in high-tempo offensive warfare. Maoist military planning envisioned a defensive military campaign fought largely on Chinese territory by "an army of rifles and millet"; the war would overstress the adversary's logistical system and mitigate the shortfalls in China's own. The doctrine of people's war, then, provided the PLA with little incentive to develop a modern logistics and supply system. Instead, each military region was left to develop and sustain its own supply infrastructure, with all the resulting inefficiency and unresponsiveness.

In 1979, the Chinese were able to move a significant quantity of troops and equipment by rail for the campaign against Vietnam. This, however, was a special case involving an overland offensive in an area having a reasonably robust rail network. Today, when Chinese security concerns seem increasingly focused on areas not contiguous to the mainland—particularly Taiwan—the PLA's limited ability to support power-projection operations could be a serious constraint on the regime's ability to employ military force to achieve its policy objectives.

Command, Control, and Communications Shortcomings. The Chinese military has suffered from enduring problems with command, control, and communications. China, like most developing countries, has lacked a modern, high-speed, high-bandwidth, redundant national communication system. However, China's rapidly growing economy is sparking significant progress in creating a more-advanced national communication backbone, and the PLA will likely benefit from these developments. Advanced communication technologies being pursued in China include fiber optics, terrestrial point-to-point microwaves, cellular telephones, communication satellites, and satellite telephones, among others.

Poor Quality of Personnel and Training. The PLA is, on the whole, poorly trained and does not offer the capability that its size alone might seem to indicate. Within the PLAAF, in particular, training is both limited and of marginal quality. A typical USAF fighter pilot will accumulate about 200 hours of flying time in a given year; his

Chinese counterpart may log 80 or so. Such limited flying time is barely enough to ensure that pilots can operate their aircraft safely; advanced operational techniques and tactics are simply impossible to learn in so little time. Although the PLAAF has organized "blue force" *Aggressor*-like units, the standard training syllabus still consists of stereotyped engagements against single, nonmaneuvering targets. The kind of free-form one-on-one or two-on-two "hassling" that is commonplace in Western air forces is virtually unknown in China, as is true joint or combined-arms training. As a result, the PLAAF has no capability to perform some missions, such as close air support, that are commonly assigned to the air arms of other nations.

Summing Up: The Chinese Military Challenge Today

China today is indisputably not a "peer competitor" of the United States; however, it is also not just another regional power. At least four important characteristics differentiate China from the "standard" regional power that appears in the "major theater war" (MTW) planning cases, such as Iraq and North Korea.

First and most important, China has nuclear weapons that can reach U.S. territory. The existence of such capabilities would weigh heavily in any possible future Sino-U.S. confrontation. For example, it is difficult to imagine that the United States would wage a largely unconstrained strategic air campaign as in Operation Desert Storm against an opponent that could wreak devastation on the American homeland, both because the United States would be concerned about crossing a threshold that might trigger Chinese nuclear retaliation and because the United States might not want to break all communication links between the Chinese leadership and its nuclear forces.

A second related point is that the PLA fields a greater variety of tactical surface-to-surface missiles than does any putative MTW adversary.[20] These systems—with different ranges, warheads, and reentry characteristics—would prove especially problematic for current and near-future U.S. ballistic missile defenses (BMD). In addition to the devastation that such a missile attack could wreak on U.S. facilities, aircraft, etc., even the *threat* of missile attack against sea and airports

---

[20]Stillion and Orletsky (1999) discusses the threat these missiles pose in detail.

might deter U.S. use of the ports and could increase absenteeism among the civilian employees of such facilities, leading to delays in U.S. strategic and intratheater force movements.

Third, the absolute size of the PLA would present challenges should the United States and China come into conflict. Under most likely circumstances, U.S. forces would at least initially find themselves greatly outnumbered, albeit by poorly trained personnel employing obsolescent systems.

Finally, China's geographic extent may make it very difficult for U.S. forces to conduct parallel attacks on the full range of targets that the USAF, in particular, anticipates striking in the course of an MTW. A comprehensive air campaign against China, by contrast, could prove to be a very long-drawn-out affair, which could greatly reduce its impact.

Thus, even today's PLA—ponderous, poorly trained, and ill-equipped as it is—presents unique and more-demanding planning and operational challenges to U.S. strategists contemplating a possible confrontation with China.[21] Beijing's ambitious modernization program could, if sustained through the first 15–20 years or so of the next century, greatly intensify those challenges.

CHINESE MILITARY MODERNIZATION

Two Avenues to Improved Capabilities

China appears to have embarked on a sustained two-tracked approach to modernizing the PLA.[22] Beijing is striving to achieve a significant degree of self-sufficiency in weapon production, but Chinese industry lacks the technological expertise to design, develop, and produce everything that the PLA needs. As a result, China has been forced to look to foreign countries—principally Russia but also Israel, France, and other Western states—to obtain military hardware. In these dealings with foreigners, the Chinese have two differ-

---

[21]This, of course, should not be read as a *prediction* that such a conflict will occur.

[22]This path—mixing indigenous production with arms purchases abroad—may not result from a deliberate strategic choice. Instead, it may simply be the outcome of disputes between the military, which wants weapons that work, and the defense industries, which argue that China should not be dependent on imports.

ent but related goals. First, they are endeavoring to fill pressing near-term military needs. Second, and perhaps more importantly, however, they are attempting to acquire advanced military and military-related technology and know-how. The foreign purchases also represent hedges against failure of indigenous development programs.

Understanding this dual approach makes sense of what might otherwise look like a wasteful acquisition policy. As Table 3.2 shows, the Chinese are simultaneously developing home-grown weapons *and* procuring foreign weapons that seem to fill the same role—for example, KILO and *Song* diesel submarines. The KILOs will both enhance the navy's current operational capabilities and serve as a source of improved submarine technology. It is not likely that the Chinese will try to reverse-engineer the KILO entirely, but will instead borrow key technologies, such as sensors, weapons, and propulsion, for incremental incorporation into indigenous designs.

It is also important to note that the two threads are interwoven. For example, after buying about 50 Su-27 FLANKER fighters from Russia, the Chinese have embarked on building additional aircraft from Sukhoi-supplied kits. Eventually, they plan to transition to building the aircraft more or less from scratch, with only the engines and a few other components being imported. In this way, the PLAAF may eventually field a force of up to 300 FLANKERS.[23]

Table 3.2

"Redundant" Chinese Development and
Acquisition Programs

System	Building	Buying
Advanced fighter	J-10	Su-27
Diesel attack submarine	*Song*	KILO
Destroyer	*Luhu, Luhai*	*Sovremenny*
Advanced surface-to-air missile (SAM)	HQ-9	SA-10

---

[23]The Chinese-built variant will probably be referred to as the J-11 and will reportedly be 70 percent of Chinese manufacture. See "Beijing Builds Su-27 Fighters from Russian Kits" (1998).

Chinese Military Modernization: Buying Abroad[24]

Varied Appetite, Modest Means. China has been an active if restrained buyer of modern weapons on the world market. The PLA's shopping list has been varied—Table 3.3 lists some of Beijing's reported recent purchases—but the pace, relative to China's financial resources, has been modest. Although the Chinese government reportedly has about $140 billion in foreign reserves, it has imported a total of only about $3 billion (1990 dollars) in weapons over the five-year period from 1990 to 1994. (Gill and Kim, 1995, p. 100.) The financial impact of these purchases has been further reduced by China's insistence on using barter to pay for significant portions of many arms deals, particularly those with Russia's hard-pressed defense industry.[25]

In addition to these purchases, China is pursuing, or has been offered, a number of other advanced weapons and systems, some of which will almost certainly find their way into Beijing's arsenal. For example, Israel and Russia are building a prototype airborne early warning aircraft—similar to the U.S. Airborne Warning and Control System—combining the Beriev A-50 airframe and the Israeli *Phalcon* radar system; China is an obvious likely customer for this system. (See Novichkov and Taverna, 1997, p. 27.) China is also reportedly acquiring some quantity of the X-31 export version of the very-long-range, Mach 2+ Russian Kh-31 air-to-air/air-to-surface missile.[26] Russian Il-78 CANDID tanker aircraft have also reportedly been discussed. The Chinese navy has also long been interested in acquiring an aircraft carrier; *Jane's Fighting Ships 1997–98* alleges that Beijing has contracted with a Russian firm to design a carrier to PLAN specifications and that fabrication of long-lead components has already begun in a Chinese shipyard. (Sharpe, 1997, p. 116.)

---

[24]It is important to exercise some caution in describing China's acquisitions of foreign weapons, since many "sales" reported in various media—particularly in the Taiwanese press—are speculative, to say the least. We have tried to confine our discussion to purchases, or expressions of Chinese interest, that can be verified through reasonably reliable sources.

[25]Reports indicate that the barter included "an enormous amount of canned fruit" and "one million cigarette lighters" were included as partial payment to Russia for weapon purchases. (See Gill and Kim, 1995, p. 58 and FBIS, 1996.)

[26]See "China and India are expected to become . . ." (1997), p. 17.

Table 3.3

Reported Chinese Arms Purchases

Type	System	Source	Qty	Notes
Fighter	Su-27 FLANKER	Russia	50+	Chinese will build more from kits, ultimately produce
Destroyer	*Sovremenny*	Russia	2	Vessels originally ordered by Russian navy
Submarine	KILO 877EKM	Russia	2	Export version
Submarine	KILO 636	Russia	2	First sale of Russian navy version
SAM	SA-10 GRUMBLE	Russia	?	Mobile and fixed variants
SAM	SA-15 GAUNTLET	Russia	15	Advanced terminal-defense SAM
Radar	Searchwater	UK	6–8	Advanced air- and sea-surveillance radar
Radar	Improved *Zhuk*	Russia	150–200	Advanced radar for F-8, F-10
Helicopter	Ka-28 HELIX	Russia	12	Ship-based antisubmarine warfare helicopter
Helicopter	*Dauphin*	France	?	Multipurpose helicopter
Helicopter	Mi-17	Russia	28+	
Air-to-air missile	*Aspide*	Italy	?	Radar-guided; similar to U.S. Sparrow
Antiship missile	SS-N-22/3M80 SUNBURN/ *Moskit*	Russia	?	Supersonic sea-skimmer to equip *Sovremenny*
Airlift	Il-76 CANDID	Russia	?	Heavy-lift transport

Finally, China has reportedly attempted to purchase numerous systems and technologies without success, at least so far, including

- The Russian R-77 (AA-12) ADDER, comparable to the U.S. Advanced Medium-Range Air-to-Air Missile (AMRAAM), as a beyond-visual-range "fire-and-forget" radar-guided air-to-air missile
- Radar surveillance satellite technology from Canada and elsewhere

- Su-30MK advanced multirole variant of the FLANKER[27]
- Tu-22M BACKFIRE bombers
- SS-18 ICBMs and/or related technology from Ukraine.

Operational Worries. In many cases, China has achieved only limited operational success with systems purchased from abroad. For example, there have been reports of maintenance and training difficulties with the PLAN's KILOs (Chen, 1997). Many of these difficulties can be attributed to the lack of Chinese operational expertise and China's disinterest in purchasing the crew-training packages that are typically part of international weapon deals. The Chinese have often bought training for only a small number of personnel with the apparent expectation that this cadre would suffice to train the necessary additional troops. Likewise, the PLA has tended to pay for only minimal training for maintenance and support personnel, with predictable results.[28] This approach has resulted in a dismal operational readiness rate for many newly acquired systems.

Before drawing profound conclusions about Chinese incompetence, however, two points should be made. First, almost all military organizations experience "growing pains" when asked to absorb new weapons and technologies; the PLA is by no mean alone in suffering from difficulties in so doing. When the USAF transitioned from the F-4 to the F-15 as its primary air-superiority fighter, for example, it took several years for training syllabi and tactics to catch up with the radically different capabilities of the new platform. And new systems in the U.S. military typically suffer from depressed readiness rates for several years after their introduction until maintenance procedures have been fully developed and spares pipelines have been filled— that is, as the weapons "mature." This occurs despite the plentiful support from the many contractors typically involved in a major Pentagon procurement program.

---

[27]With orders from India and Indonesia for the Su-30MK on the books, Russia may find it increasingly difficult to refuse if China persists in pursuing the aircraft. On March 2, 1999, the Hong Kong *Standard* reported that China was "negotiating with Russia to buy Su-30 fighters . . . ." (Fong and Lee, 1999.)

[28]Indeed, some Russian sources have expressed puzzlement over China's desire to invest billions in hardware without making the relatively minor additional commitment needed to train an adequate number of appropriate personnel. See Chen (1997) and "China Should Receive Its Third 'Kilo' by November" (1997,) p. 16.

It should also be recalled that these purchases fill a second need beyond any operational requirement: serving as technology demonstrators for Chinese industry. Any operational difficulties, while undoubtedly worrisome to the PLA leadership, may be secondary to the exploitation of these systems for technologies, techniques, and components that can be incorporated into China's own arms production. It is to these domestic initiatives that we now turn our attention.

Chinese Military Modernization: Building at Home

Although the goal has proven elusive, China has long sought self-sufficiency in military production. The first jet aircraft built in China was the MiG-15, and the J-5 version of the MiG-17 became the first modern fighter put into serial production in China in 1956. Similarly, the Chinese began building the T-59 variant of the Soviet T-54 tank in the late 1950s. By the 1970s, Chinese industry was producing a fairly broad range of weapons and systems, including aircraft, ships, armored vehicles, artillery, and submarines.

A Mixed Track Record. China has enjoyed imperfect success in its various weapon development programs. Most of its efforts to date have focused on learning to manufacture systems, via either reverse engineering or licensed production, that were initially imported. Table 3.4 lists some of these aircraft and vehicles, as well as the approximate length of time it took from when the PLA first acquired

Table 3.4

Selected Chinese Arms Production Programs

Chinese Name	Original	Type	Date Acquired	Entered Production	Elapsed Time (years)
T-59	T-54	Tank	1953(?)	1957	4
J-6	MiG-19	Fighter	1958	1963	5
J-7	MiG-21	Fighter	1961	1967	6
Y-7	An-24	Transport	1976	1984	8
H-6	Tu-16	Bomber	1957	1968	11
Z-9	*Dauphin*	Helicopter	1980	1992	12
Y-8	An-28	Transport	1969	1986	17

the item for it to enter production. Given the timelines shown, it is no mystery why the PLA finds itself fielding mostly obsolescent weapons: Even when the system being copied is top of the line when the process begins, the design will be 10 or more years old by the time the Chinese version enters service.

The Chinese have demonstrated considerable patience with their development projects, pursuing incremental upgrades and improvements even after the basic design has exceeded its useful life. This can result in systems that are, as one analyst said of the J-6, "the most highly perfected, obsolescent aircraft in the world." (Allen, Krumel, and Pollack, 1995, p. 148.) The same observation would probably hold true for the J-7, a MiG-21 derivative whose most recent variant only entered production in 1989, 30 years after the original FISHBED was brought into Soviet service.[29]

China's indigenous development programs have not been limited to reverse-engineering Soviet designs; Beijing has also fostered numerous undertakings of greater originality, with similar histories of mixed results.

Nuclear Weapons. The development of nuclear weapons certainly ranks among modern China's greatest technological accomplishments. Despite some initial technical help from the Soviets, China's development of nuclear weapons was based almost entirely on indigenous resources and expertise. Even after the withdrawal of all Soviet technical assistance by 1960, China still detonated its first fission weapon in October 1964, only eight years after beginning construction of its first research reactor. Perhaps even more impressively, China's first thermonuclear test took place just two-and-a-half years later, in June 1967. And, unlike the first U.S. hydrogen bomb, the Chinese device was not the size of railroad tank car; it was an air-dropped bomb.

Ballistic Missiles. Ballistic missiles have been another area in which the Chinese have demonstrated significant technical competence. As noted above, the PLA has a large and varied inventory of missiles, from the short range DF-11 to the DF-5 ICBM. Recently, China

---

[29]China continues to work on updated versions of the J-7. The J-7FS reportedly first flew on June 5, 1998; according to reports, it features upgraded avionics, a new engine, and GPS access.

indigenously developed the technology for solid-propellant missiles and has advanced to the point where its road-mobile, short-range, solid-propellant missiles are sought-after export items. While it has not yet fielded multiple-warhead missiles, China succeeded in launching multiple satellites from a single booster in 1984. This suggests that China may not be very far from acquiring the technical prerequisites for MIRVed payloads.

Cruise Missiles. Cruise missiles, primarily of the antiship variety, have also figured prominently in China's repertoire. Beginning with the HY-1—based on the Soviet P-15 (SS-N-2A STYX)—which entered service in 1974, China has developed a series of increasingly sophisticated weapons. Current programs may include

- The YJ-1, or C-801, has a solid propellant booster and is similar in appearance to the French *Exocet*, reportedly reflecting similar design requirements rather than reverse engineering.

- The YJ-2 (C-802), which may be entering service now, replaces the solid propellant sustainer motor of its predecessor with a turbojet and as a result has a much longer range (120 km versus 40 km). (Periscope, 1998.)

- An even longer-range version (180 km) of the YJ-2 is reportedly under development, as is a land-attack version that incorporates a GPS guidance system and terrain contour-matching.[30]

Two new long-range land-attack cruise missiles are also being worked on, and one or both will likely enter service after 2000. There are reports of extensive Israeli and Russian involvement in these programs, including assertions that the Chinese hired an entire cruise missile R&D team from Russia in 1995 (Blank, 1997). Both air- and sea-launched variants are anticipated.[31] Beijing's efforts in this area may be expected to benefit from China's acquisition of a number of SS-N-22/3M80 SUNBURN/*Moskit* missiles to equip its *Sovremenny* destroyers.

Nuclear Submarines. The Chinese have also invested heavily in nuclear submarine technology, building at least five *Han*-class nuclear attack submarines (SSNs) and one *Xia*-class SSBN. All have

---

[30]Lennox and Starr (1996) and Bowen and Shepard (1996).

[31]U.S. Department of Defense (n.d.), p. 4.

been plagued with problems with their power plants, although the *Han* fleet has reportedly been significantly more active in the mid-1990s than heretofore (Sharpe, 1997, p. 114).

The PLAN is currently developing two new nuclear submarines that are slated to enter service after the turn of the century. The Type 093 SSN is believed to be comparable to the Soviet VICTOR III class and will benefit from Russian quieting technology, as will the Type 094 "boomer."[32]

SAMs. As in other areas, China's first forays into SAM development involved reverse engineering Soviet systems. Today, China fields a number of indigenously manufactured SAMs both on land and at sea; most are still evolutionary developments of foreign missiles, as shown in Table 3.5.

The current centerpiece of the PLA's SAM development is the HQ-9, which is reputed to be a highly modified version of the SA-10 GRUMBLE which the Chinese purchased from Russia earlier this decade. The HQ-9 is alleged to incorporate guidance and propulsion technology from the U.S. *Patriot*, which Israel supposedly provided to Beijing (Fulgham, 1993b).[33] The *Patriot* know-how is thought to serve mainly to enhance the HQ-9s capabilities against ballistic missiles and may make the system considerably more attractive to potential export customers (Fulgham, 1993a).

New Fighter Aircraft: The J-10, FC-1, and XXJ. Currently, China is developing at least two new fighter aircraft. The J-10 is a high-performance single-engine fighter with a clear family lineage back to the canceled Israeli *Lavi* and, in turn, to the Lockheed-Martin F-16. Israeli assistance has reportedly been centered on avionics, radar, and flight controls, and Israel may have supplied a *Lavi* prototype as well. The engine is reputed to be the same AL-31 that powers the Su-27. After a prolonged gestation, the first flight of the J-10 occurred in March 1998, and the aircraft is expected to be in PLAAF service by 2005.

---

[32]"Russia Helps China take new SSNs into silent era" (1997).

[33]If such a transfer did indeed occur, it could also have helped the Chinese develop ballistic-missile reentry vehicles that could defeat current and future U.S. anti-missile systems.

Table 3.5

Chinese SAM Systems

Name	Type	Based On
HQ-2	Medium-to-high altitude, radar guided	SA-2 GUIDELINE
HQ-7	Low-to-medium altitude, radar guided	*Crotale*
HN-5	Man-portable, infrared guided	SA-7 GRAIL
QW-1	Advanced man-portable, infrared guided	FIM-92 Stinger
HQ-61	Low-to-medium altitude, radar guided	None
LY-60	Low-to-medium altitude, radar guided	None
HQ-9	Advanced all-altitude, radar guided	SA-10 GRUMBLE, Patriot

The FC-1 is a lightweight, single-engine, multirole fighter being developed primarily for export, with Pakistan as the main customer. Some reports indicate that the PLAAF will buy some number of the aircraft as part of a "high-low" mix strategy with the more capable Su-27 and J-10.

Finally, it has recently been reported that another new fighter, the XXJ, is in the early stages of development with a target service entry date of about 2015. The XXJ is assessed as a twin-engine fighter in the Su-27/F-15 class with multirole capabilities and some low-observable characteristics.

Other Programs

The Chinese are also pursuing a number of other defense-related development efforts that could reach fruition in the early part of the next century.

Space. China is one of the world's space-faring nations, with a demonstrated capability to launch and operate Earth-orbiting spacecraft. Since 1970, China has successfully flown a variety of satellites, including communications, meteorological, and surveillance systems. In addition, China today offers commercial launch services to a variety of customers and may even conduct manned spaceflights in the next few years. While China's space program appears to be in something of a hiatus—only five Chinese spacecraft are operational on orbit as of this writing—this by no means reflects a lack of interest in space-related technology.

For example, China is developing a new generation of photoreconnaissance satellites, the FSW-3 series, which will provide 1-meter resolution, and the Chinese National Remote Sensing Center also receives imagery from U.S. LANDSAT, French SPOT, Israeli EROS, and Russian remote-sensing satellites (Stokes, 1997). Although the Chinese have yet to launch a radar-surveillance satellite of their own, the National Remote Sensing Center does receive downlinks from the Canadian RADARSAT platform.

China is also well-positioned to be part of the emerging era of widespread commercial exploitation of space. With its large economy and foreign-exchange reserves and its relatively advanced technological base, China is participating in a number of international space ventures, including the *Iridium* and *Globalstar* satellite communication systems. China's financial resources could also make its military a major consumer of "pay-for-play" commercial remote sensing systems such as Quick Bird, Orbview, EROS, and advanced SPOT, which will come into service in the next few years and offer on-demand high-resolution multispectral imagery. So, the Chinese may be able to derive many of the advantages of space exploitation without building or launching a single satellite of their own.

The Chinese may also benefit as something of a free rider on space capabilities developed by other parties. The U.S. GPS and Russian GLONASS systems, for example, appear to be evolving into global geolocation utilities, freely accessible to all comers. China is reportedly already exploiting GPS/GLONASS to improve the accuracy of its ballistic missiles.

Finally, there is an extensive Chinese literature on the importance of antisatellite weapons in future wars, along with evidence that the PLA is interested in fielding such weapons. One likely candidate would be a ground-based laser; one analyst has concluded that "China has the basic technologies needed to move to more advanced R&D stages" of such an antisatellite system (Stokes, 1997).

Directed Energy. China is devoting significant attention to R&D in the area of directed energy. While little has been disclosed publicly about such efforts, Chinese writings suggest that Beijing is working in a variety of areas, including high-powered microwave weapons, as well as lasers. The Chinese have also conducted extensive research on electronic countermeasures.

Information Warfare. It is perhaps most difficult of all to say anything useful about PLA work on offensive and defensive information warfare. After all, Beijing does not have to marshal its information warfare brigades for parades or maneuvers, and new information warfare weapons, unlike new fighters or frigates, are invisible to overhead observation. However, the evidence that has come to light is suggestive of great interest.

Chinese writing on information warfare–related issues is quite copious; much of it focuses on information warfare as a way for a "weaker" power to defeat a "superior" adversary. The Chinese have explicitly discussed the perceived vulnerabilities of some U.S. military information systems. Indeed, one Chinese-language book on Internet hacking is full of screen shots depicting successful penetrations into computers in the U.S. ".af.mil" domain.

Summing Up: The Chinese Military in 2015

It is not possible to make any definitive pronouncements on the shape of the Chinese military in 2015. There are too many variables—such as China's economic growth rate, its political evolution, and the overall East Asian security environment—that affect the final result. We can, however, by assessing the PLA's current shortcomings and examining its modernization efforts, draw some tentative insights about what China might or must do to create a modern military in the next two decades.

At present, China is not on a trajectory to become a global military competitor to the United States by 2015. Unless the U.S. permits its own military power to atrophy dramatically, there is little chance that China will emerge as a true global military competitor in the next 15 to 20 years. Beijing finds itself so far behind the United States in so many dimensions that nothing short of a sustained and total national mobilization would permit the PLA to make up so much ground so fast, and we see no evidence that such an all-out effort is under way or even likely.

China could, however, emerge as a formidable power, one that might be labeled a *multidimensional regional competitor*. As such, China would possess more than just a big army; it could credibly

- exercise sea denial with respect to the seas contiguous to China
- contest aerospace superiority in a sustained way in areas contiguous to China's borders

- threaten U.S. operating locations in East Asia with a variety of long-range strike assets
- challenge U.S. information dominance
- pose a strategic nuclear threat to the United States.

We believe the following would have to occur for China to accomplish this:

- Chinese defense expenditures would have to continue to increase in real terms.
- The PLA would have to be willing and able to trade quantity for quality.
- The PLA would have to open itself to doctrinal, operational, and tactical innovation.
- The Chinese defense industrial base would have to continue to develop and mature.

Increased Defense Spending. In the 1990s, Chinese defense budgets have begun growing in real terms after more than a decade of stasis or decline. Satisfying the PLA's manifold needs—for new equipment, additional training, better maintenance, and so on—will require that these increases continue for the foreseeable future.

Through the 1990s, China's military expenditures have grown at roughly the same rate as the Chinese economy as a whole, so that defense spending as a proportion of GNP has remained more or less constant.[34] If China's economy continues to grow at anything like the rates seen over the last 10 to 20 years—and economists differ on the likelihood of this—the PLA should be able to accomplish a great deal without creating an undue burden on the Chinese economy as a whole.[35]

---

[34]The year-to-year increase in real defense spending in 1997 somewhat exceeded the increase in GNP. Most observers, however, believe this resulted more from unexpectedly low inflation than from a change in Chinese government policy.

[35]As of this writing, the effects on China of the ongoing Asian economic crisis remain uncertain. So far, Beijing's large economy and reserves of foreign exchange have helped China avoid a dramatic downturn, such as those that have struck Indonesia, South Korea, and other "tigers." How long these ill winds can blow without seriously buffeting China is an open question.

Trading Quantity for Quality. Put most simply, the PLA is too manpower intensive. With the requirement to defend an extensive land border against the might of the Soviet Union gone, there is little compelling military justification for fielding a 3-million-man army. Getting the maximum modernization "bang" for each budget "buck" will demand a significant reduction in the overall size of the PLA.

The PLA will also need to reduce the bewildering confusion of types of systems in its inventory. By fielding, as it does, numerous versions of tanks, aircraft, and other equipment, the PLA forgoes economies of scale in training and maintenance, as well as in production. The need to rely on so many disparate suppliers, foreign and domestic, has created this situation, as has the political imperative to provide adequate contractual support to the many SOEs engaged in defense manufacture. Larger defense budgets will have little impact if the money must continue to be spread across so many programs and if logistic and training programs remain fragmented and inadequate.

Pursuing Innovation. As it modernizes its hardware, the Chinese military must also update its software: the doctrine, operational art, and tactics that govern its functioning and the training that converts recruits into professional men-at-arms.

Although improvements are being made, such as the utilization of "blue teams," the PLA's approach to training is highly stylized and falls far short of the standards of most Western powers. To the extent that the divergent approaches and standards represent a simple extension of the difference in warfighting styles between China and, say, the United States, they are, of course, valid. However, when an Su-27 pilot is being trained only in one-on-one tail-chase intercepts against nonmaneuvering targets, he is being trained to waste his airplane. New equipment implies new concepts, and the Chinese will need to foment a doctrinal revolution to complement the technological one if the billions to be spent on modern weapons are to pay off in enhanced capabilities.

In particular, it is almost commonplace to observe that power projection is an inherently joint undertaking. If the Chinese wish to secure Taiwan by brute force, protect Beijing's proclaimed interests in the South China Sea, or contest control of the vital sea lanes of the southern Pacific and Indian oceans, the PLA must become competent in joint operations. Today, a "joint exercise" in China most often means that the army, navy, and air force are in the same general area training independently. This must change dramatically if China is to achieve its potential as a military power.

Mature the Defense Industrial Base. Finally, an effective and thoroughgoing modernization of the PLA will rest on a well developed indigenous arms industry. Accomplishing this maturation will depend on many things:

- rationalization of the industry so that inefficient producers fall out

- selective integration of reliable foreign partners who bring key resources—capital or specific technologies—to the table

- development of an adequately educated, technologically competent workforce[36]

- promulgation of a strategic R&D vision that focuses scarce resources on areas where China has a pressing need—jet engines for example—and areas that appear critical to the conduct of future wars, such as microelectronics and information processing.

---

[36]The disparity between China and the United States may be illustrated by the following: Each year, U.S. colleges and universities award three times as many bachelor's degrees as their Chinese counterparts, even though China's population is roughly five times that of the United States.

Chapter Four

U.S. POLICY OPTIONS

Given China's potential to pose a political-military challenge to the United States, as well as the uncertainty about the future course it will follow, how should the United States deal with it? What U.S. actions can both encourage China to follow a more cooperative policy and prepare the United States for the possibility that it will not? To the extent that these two objectives may come into conflict, how should the U.S. strike a balance between them? This chapter first looks at overall U.S. policy toward China and then considers some specific implications for the U.S. Air Force.

CURRENT U.S. POLICY TOWARD CHINA: INCONSISTENT "ENGAGEMENT"

Engagement as a Policy

The fundamental policy of the Bush and, after some peregrinations, the Clinton administrations has been one of "engagement," although one could argue that neither administration followed a "pure" engagement policy and that each tended to hedge its bets in certain ways, although the steps taken in this regard were often not presented in this context.

In principle, engagement seeks to maintain and enhance relations with China as much as possible in the various policy realms. Strictly speaking, engagement is a tactic rather than a policy: It refers to the means—increased contact and a denser network of relationships—rather than the objectives. However, as we shall see, it in practice embodies some assumptions about how such a tactic will achieve certain objectives.

Economically, it seeks normal trade relations by granting "most favored nation" (MFN) trade status, reducing the number of sensitive goods and technologies covered by export controls, simplifying the export control procedures, allowing Chinese companies to operate relatively freely in the United States, and facilitating Chinese entry into such international economic organizations as the WTO.

Politically, engagement seeks to maximize bilateral ties while keeping any disputes at as low a level as possible. It tries to bring China into the various multilateral arms control regimes dealing with weapons of mass destruction, proliferation, arms trade, etc., and into other international regimes dealing with such issues as humans rights (such as the International Covenant on Civil and Political Rights). It attempts to involve China in the solution of regional issues, such as Korea.

Militarily, it seeks to increase military-to-military relations of various sorts. Obviously, this implies the avoidance of conflict with China. Under this policy, the United States would also promote China's participation in regional security organizations, such as the ASEAN Regional Forum (ARF).[1]

Rationale of the Engagement Policy

Engagement appears to have two variants with regard to the underlying assumptions concerning what the result of China's enmeshment in the international system will be. One variant assumes that, over time, China's involvement in the international economic and political system will socialize its leaders into international norms of behavior while increasing their stake in the current system. (This is the "acculturation" possibility discussed in Chapter Two.) According to this theory, the more China is integrated into the international system, the less likely China will be to use force, as this would threaten its interests. President Clinton noted in May of 1997, when he advocated renewing China's MFN status, that continued trade would "bring China into the family of nations."[2] Similarly, James Baker

---

[1]ARF is ASEAN's associated security organization. It includes the members of ASEAN and important external states, such as China, the United States, the European Union, and Russia. For more on ARF, see Wortzel (1995).

[2]"Clinton: Extend China's Favored Trade Status" (1997).

called for deepening Beijing's economic links with the outside world, claiming that foreign trade and investment are the best guarantees of China's stability (Baker, 1996). This view assumes that, although China's government might remain authoritarian, China would still act as a prudent and responsible member of the international system, once it became accustomed to the current international "rules of the game" and understood the benefits that the current system can bestow (i.e., political-military stability, international trade opportunities, access to foreign capital and resources).

A stronger variant of the engagement rationale would hold that, in addition to the restraining effects of enmeshment in the international system, increased Chinese interaction with the outside world will also facilitate the democratization of China. And not only will a democratic China be good in itself, it will also be less likely to come into conflict with the United States. This argument holds that China's economic growth and social change will promote prodemocracy forces, including growth of the middle class, a desire for rule by law, and other elements. James Dorn of the Cato Institute argues that "free markets foster economic development and provide individuals with the means to liberate themselves from the state." (Dorn, 1996.)[3] This view has won over many critics of China's current regime. As House Majority Leader Richard Armey noted,

> In my heart, I would like to oppose most-favored-nation status for China as a way of expressing the deep repugnance I feel toward the tyranny of Beijing, but intellectually I believe that continued normal trade relations are best for the people of China today and offer the best prospect for liberating them in years to come. (Armey, 1997.)

In confronting the desire to "punish" China for human rights violations, engagement argues that confronting China on human rights issues would provoke a backlash that would inhibit, rather than increase, the chances for political reform.

---

[3]This view is widely held. David Lampton (1994, p. 12) notes that the United States can promote its values by fueling the development of a middle class in China through trade. James R. Lilley (1994, p. 37) similarly argues that a major engine of democracy and freedom is U.S. political and economic engagement. The best theoretical exposition of this point of view is Friedman (1982).

The Taiwan Issue in the Context of Engagement

⌐The status of Taiwan is a major potential difficulty for the policy of engagement. While a U.S. administration can agree that Taiwan is part of China and oppose *de jure* Taiwanese independence, it will find it politically impossible simply to abandon Taiwan. Rather, the United States has, in various statements, expressed "an abiding interest and concern that any resolution [of the Taiwan question] be peaceful."[4] Pursuant to this general approach, the Clinton administration responded to Chinese saber rattling (missile and other military exercises directed against Taiwan) in March 1996 by sending two carrier battle groups into the waters around Taiwan. Thus, while the U.S. and Chinese positions overlap (both would allow for peaceful reunification) there is grounds for a potential conflict as well, should China decide to use force to bring about reunification.⌐

One way to avoid this potential problem would be for the United States *actively* to promote the peaceful reunification of Taiwan and China, attempting to influence both sides toward a reunification agreement, on whatever terms might be feasible. (Since such a policy would seek mainly to remove the Taiwan issue as a source of possible conflict in the future, the policy could be indifferent to the terms on which this was accomplished. As far as engagement is concerned, the terms could range from the current PRC position of "one country, two systems" all the way to a notion of "shared sovereignty" leaving each side pretty much free to pursue its own interests as it saw fit.) Of course, the terms would have to be favorable enough to Taiwan that the agreement could be plausibly regarded as voluntary on its part, although it is unclear whether this is possible. At present, it is unclear whether the engagement policy, as practiced by the current administration, contains such an element.

Limitations of Engagement as a Policy

As noted, engagement is more properly a tactic than an actual policy, although it does aim at a more or less clear objective. However, it is silent on what should be done when actions come into conflict with

---

[4]Citation is from President Reagan's Statement on United States Arms Sales to Taiwan, August 17, 1982, reprinted in Harding (1992), p. 386.

U.S. interests and goals (e.g., although engagement is intended to acculturate the Chinese leadership to various global norms, such as nonproliferation, it does not indicate how the United States should respond when China acts in opposition to them). At most, it says what *shouldn't* be done, i.e., the United States should *not* react by cutting off ties to China, reducing the level of diplomatic interaction, imposing economic sanctions, etc. In principle, other U.S. reactions would have to be considered in the light of the possibility that they would cause China to reduce relations with the United States.[5] However, in practice, at least in recent years, it has been the United States that has debated whether its relations with China should be cut back when the Chinese have behaved in ways antithetical to U.S. objectives and interests.

Thus, engagement appears to rule out the typical low-level actions that the United States takes to express its displeasure with foreign state behavior of which it disapproves. As a result, there have been cases—for example, the Bush administration's suspension of most diplomatic exchanges with Beijing in the aftermath of Tiananmen—when it has proved impossible to follow its precepts. Similarly, the Clinton administration was unwilling to allow China to join the WTO under the favorable terms it demanded and has even threatened economic sanctions over some issues, such as the Chinese government's failure to protect the intellectual property rights of U.S. corporations. In addition, the post-Tiananmen sanctions, which prohibit the sale of weapon systems and other military equipment (such as spare parts) to China, remain in effect. In early 1999, the Clinton administration prohibited the sale of a communication satellite to a Singapore-based company because of its ties to the PLA.

Criticisms of Engagement Policy

Engagement is open to several criticisms that have led to a search for an alternative. As noted above, engagement, generally speaking, does not really deal with the question of how to respond to Chinese behavior considered unacceptable.

---

[5]For example, one could argue that allowing Taiwanese president Lee Teng-hui to make an unofficial visit to the United States in 1995 did not violate the "letter" of the engagement policy; however, it may have been inconsistent with its spirit, since it could have led the Chinese to reduce contacts with the United States.

With respect to human rights violations, the argument is that, to paraphrase Franklin Roosevelt, "the only cure for the ills of engagement is more engagement," i.e., that engagement itself has the best chance of promoting respect for human rights and democratization generally. While this means that the Chinese leadership is not "punished" for Tiananmen-like behavior, proponents of engagement could respond that the ultimate objective is still better served, i.e., that Chinese behavior is more likely to evolve in the desired direction under the influence of personal contact, enhanced communication, etc. (which engagement fosters) than under the threat or actuality of "punishment," which could involve severing communication channels. The occasional Chinese attacks on "peaceful evolution"—the supposed U.S. policy of using cultural influences to subvert communism in China—could be seen as (no doubt inadvertent) support for this argument.

Nevertheless, it may be difficult to obtain domestic consensus for a policy that bars any effective expression of American moral outrage after Tiananmen-like events. Even though the Bush administration cut off high-level public contacts with the Chinese leadership in 1989, the administration's continuing secret contacts at the level of the national security advisor led, when these contacts were revealed publicly, to attacks on it for "coddling" Beijing.

With respect to other issues, moreover, engagement offers no guidance. Thus, when China sells sensitive nuclear-related materials to Pakistan or engages in unfair trade practices, engagement merely counsels that economic or diplomatic sanctions *not* be applied in retaliation; it has no positive suggestions for dealing with the problem.[6]

More fundamentally, engagement rests on an assumption—that continued contact will eventually affect Chinese behavior in a positive direction—that is far from certain. In the meantime, it helps China develop economically and technologically, thus creating the

---

[6]One could argue that narrow sanctions, e.g., a trade ban imposed on the specific companies involved in selling sensitive materials, *would* be consistent with engagement. However, such sanctions would be hard to impose and enforce and would be easy to circumvent, given the ability of the guilty parties in China to use front companies or other types of cut-outs.

base for future military strength. Thus, should the assumption prove incorrect, engagement will merely have helped China become a more-threatening adversary in the future. Even if the leadership is temporarily willing to abide by U.S.-supported norms of international behavior—to secure the advantages of engagement—there is no guarantee that its acquiescence will continue once China's comprehensive national power has been enhanced. At that point, China may feel confident of its ability to make its way in the world without economic or other relations with the United States or may believe that its importance in world affairs is now so great that the United States will have no choice but to seek good relations with it.

CONTAINMENT AS AN ALTERNATIVE POLICY

Substance of a Containment Policy

Some have suggested that a containment policy would be a more realistic way to deal with the prospect of a powerful China in the future. The goal of a policy of containment would be to avoid an increase in China's power relative to that of the United States. This would include efforts to slow down China's economic growth in general, as this is the fundamental basis for national power, and to prevent an upgrading of its military capabilities in particular. It would also include efforts to limit the expansion of China's influence beyond its present borders.

The goal of containment would be to prevent an increase in China's power. Containment assumes that allowing China to expand its influence will not diminish its appetite but rather embolden its leaders, making an eventual clash with the United States even more likely. And the more powerful China is, the more stressing this clash will be for the United States. Thus, even modest moves on China's part should be resisted.

Under a containment policy, all elements of the U.S.-China relationship would be subordinate to the goal of preventing the growth of China's power. Thus, the United States would work to limit foreign trade and investment in China and in particular prevent the transfer of any technology that might aid China's military. Preventing the unification of Taiwan's capital and technology with mainland China's manpower and resources would be especially important. In particular, the United States would announce that *any* attack against the island would be met with force, thereby encouraging independence forces on Taiwan. The United States would try to increase its military access to the region to be in a position to thwart any potential aggression.

Allies would play a particularly important role. The United States would have to strengthen existing bilateral alliances and focus them toward the emerging China threat. It would also need to forge new, anti-China alliances to build up the militaries of Vietnam, Indonesia, India, and other potential security partners in the region. Without allies, containment would be far less effective, as China could find other markets and other sources of investment. In particular, the United States would have to try to convince its allies (and, to the extent possible, other potential sources of advanced military equipment and technology) to impose limits on their exports to China, to keep advanced militarily related technology out of its hands.

The Assumptions on Which Containment Would Be Based: Realist Theory

A policy of containment would assume that serious conflicts of interest with China were highly likely and that the United States should both demonstrate its resolve to deter China from challenging it and take steps to prepare for conflicts should deterrence fail. The argument for containment contains two predominant strands. First, it accepts the lessons of realist international relations theory, which argues that rising powers in general are likely to assert themselves on the world scene and to challenge the predominant power; this challenge often results in a general systemic war that determines whether the predominant power retains its status or is replaced by the challenger. Second, it reads Chinese history to say that China, given its historical tradition of regional dominance and its view of itself as having been victimized by the "West" during a century and a half of "national humiliation," will seek to become at least a regional hegemon in East Asia and to challenge what it sees as American "hegemony" and the current system of international norms, which it sees as biased in favor of those who created it. Furthermore, proponents of containment would be likely to argue either that China, given its political tradition of imperial rule, is unlikely to democratize, or that, even if it did, its policy would not become less bellicose, since it would have to respond to the nationalist passions of the populace.[7]

Difficulties and Disadvantages of Containment

At present, containment would be a very difficult policy to implement: First, it would be hard to obtain a domestic consensus to subordinate other policy goals (including, most prominently, trade) to dealing with a Chinese threat that is as yet, to say the least, far from manifest. It would be difficult to mobilize national energies on the basis of predictions that are not only extremely pessimistic but necessarily uncertain as well. Also, a policy of containment might well cause the Chinese to become more hostile than they otherwise would be. Indeed, many argue that the underlying prediction of Sino-U.S. hostility would be self-fulfilling, leading to a conflict where none would otherwise have occurred. Whether or not it would make conflict more likely, containment would appear to eliminate the possibility that Chinese policy would evolve in a favorable direction.

Second, to be effective, containment would require the wholehearted cooperation of regional allies and most of the other advanced industrial countries of the world. Again, such cooperation would be difficult to obtain: Allies in Western Europe may not believe that even an aggressive, rising China poses a threat to them, while allies in the region may not easily be convinced that such a hard policy toward China is necessary. In addition, whatever leverage over Chinese policies the United States attained by means of the engagement policy (with respect to such issues as, e.g., sales of missiles or technology related to weapons of mass destruction) would be lost. China might feel that it was freer to use its local military superiority vis-à-vis its neighbors to exert pressure on them, since the benefits of better relations with the United States and other advanced industrial nations were being denied it in any case.

In general, containment seems excessively fatalistic; it seems unnecessarily to resign itself to an unfavorable outcome, while overlooking the possibility that Sino-U.S. relations can perhaps evolve in a much more acceptable fashion.

---

[7]These arguments are treated at length in Chapter Two.

A "THIRD WAY"

Combining Containment with Engagement ("Congagement")

The difficulties surrounding both containment and engagement raise the question of whether some type of combination of the two policies might be possible that would preserve some of the hope of the engagement policy while hedging against its possible inability to discourage China from challenging U.S. interests and objectives. Such a "third way" policy would continue to try to bring China into the current international system while both preparing for a possible Chinese challenge to it and seeking to convince the Chinese leadership that such a challenge would be difficult to prepare and extremely risky to pursue.

The key to the success of such a policy would be keeping its elements in balance. It will need to minimize the negative effects on Chinese attitudes of steps taken to hedge against the possibility of future hostility. Many Chinese observers claim that the United States has already adopted a policy of containment toward China; it is hard to sort out to what extent this represents a true belief on their part and to what extent it is a tactic to put the United States on the psychological defensive, i.e., to place on the United States the burden of proving that it is *not* trying to contain China. Thus, determining the actual negative effect of any of these measures will be a difficult and uncertain process.

In any case, this issue suggests the importance of paying attention to the way in which this policy is presented in public; the declaratory policies that go along with these steps may influence how they are perceived in China and how they affect the evolution of Chinese behavior.

Elements of Such a Policy

"Modified Engagement." This policy would continue a great deal of the engagement policy, although modified in certain respects. In general, it would seek to enhance economic, political and cultural ties with China. In doing so, however, it would be less solicitous of Chinese sensitivities on such issues as human rights; for example, U.S. spokesmen would be more vigorous in criticizing Chinese practices, without, however, suggesting that sanctions might be applied to change them. On these issues, U.S. policy would proceed from a recognition that, as President Clinton said of its attitude toward human rights and religious freedom, China is "on the wrong side of history" and will be, sooner or later, forced to make some accommodation to the demand for a freer system of government.

A greater effort would be made to impose sanctions on specific Chinese companies that, for example, exported nuclear sensitive materials, violated U.S. export control laws, or otherwise thwarted major U.S. objectives. While the effectiveness of such a policy would be limited by an inability to understand all the interconnections and front companies involved, it might be possible, on at least some occasions, to impose real costs on Chinese corporations and individuals, which might lead to more careful behavior.

Strengthening Ties to Regional Countries. The United States would seek to strengthen its ties to the East Asian nations (including countries, like Russia, that are partly in the region), as well as to improve relations among them. The goal should be to prepare the way for closer security ties between the United States and states in the region, as well as for multilateral security arrangements, should they become necessary in the future. The underlying, but unstated, rationale of this activity would be to emphasize to China the costs of, and thereby deter, any Chinese attempt at seeking regional hegemony.

Such a policy would have many elements, among which might be

1. Attempts to enhance military-to-military relations between Japan and South Korea. Efforts could include various "confidence-building measures," such as more transparency in their respective defense plans.

2. Attempts to enhance political-military cooperation among the ASEAN states. In particular, they should be encouraged to approach the issue of their overlapping claims to the Spratly Islands and the South China Sea in a multilateral context that includes China; however, a Chinese refusal to engage multilaterally should not prevent the other states from pursuing the issue among themselves.

3. Encouragement of a Japanese-Russian rapprochement, including a settlement of the dispute over the "northern territories."

4. Enhanced military-to-military cooperation between the United States and the ASEAN states.

U.S. Military Forces. Future U.S. military forces would have to be configured in part for possible Chinese scenarios, including the defense of Taiwan. This would require attention to the warfighting requirements imposed by a possible conflict with China,[8] as well as taking steps to ensure access to facilities in the region. In general, it may not be possible or desirable to acquire bases in the traditional sense; on the other hand, joint exercises, access agreements, port visits, etc., can provide the groundwork for joint action when necessary.

The large distances of the East Asian region also suggest that longer range forces will be necessary to operate in this theater. That has major procurement implications for USAF with respect to its next generation of combat aircraft.

"Ambiguity" With Respect to Taiwan. Ultimately, any such policy must confront the question of the future of Taiwan. As opposed to engagement, whose logic seems to suggest that we actively (if quietly) promote the peaceful reunification of Taiwan with China lest the situation become the spark for a crisis that destroys the policy, this policy assumes that it is in the U.S. interest for the *status quo* to be preserved for as long as China's future path remains uncertain. This preference need not, of course, be part of U.S. policy, which would continue to emphasize the importance the United States places on a peaceful resolution of the Taiwan issue.

However, if China were to become a friendly, democratic power, U.S. policy could become more favorable to reunification; of course, under these circumstances, Taiwanese opinion might also become more favorable to reunification. On the other hand, if China were to become hostile, the United States could adopt a policy of bolstering Taiwan's *de facto* independence. This could also reflect a possible proindependence shift in Taiwanese sentiment, if China's reforms

_____

[8]Discussed in the next section.

were to stall and China were to adopt a more confrontational stance toward its neighbors and toward the United States .

The future of Taiwan depends on the interplay of two sets of forces, one of which pushes Taiwan toward independence, and the other toward incorporation into China. On the one hand, the economies of Taiwan and China are becoming more and more closely tied together in terms of trade and investment; thus, any worsening of relations will scare large sectors of the Taiwanese business community, which may pressure the government to be more accommodating to Chinese demands. The other set of forces includes the democratization of Taiwanese political life; the island's economic success; and, ultimately, the emergence of a separate sense of national identity based on those successes, the slow but steady absorption of the "mainlanders" into the indigenous population, and the "normalization" of its domestic life in political terms.[9] Assuming Taiwan completes its democratic transition successfully, its people will find it stranger and stranger that they should owe allegiance to an undemocratic leadership in Beijing.

Assumptions Behind Such a Policy

This policy would be agnostic on some of the key judgments about China's future, e.g., whether China's enmeshing in the international system will modify its long-term objectives and behavior and whether China as a rising power will inevitably challenge U.S. global leadership. The goal would be to sharpen the fundamental choice China's leadership faces—cooperating with the current international system as opposed to challenging the U.S. world role and pursuing regional hegemony—by presenting the alternatives starkly. In particular, it would seek to persuade China to avoid the mistakes of Wilhelmian Germany in the period leading up to World War I.

IMPLICATIONS FOR THE U.S. ARMED FORCES AND THE USAF IN PARTICULAR

Regardless of which overall policy the United States adopts, dealing with the long-term process of Chinese military modernization will

---

[9]It is little more than a decade since the end of the "state of emergency."

impose many requirements on the U.S. armed forces and the USAF in particular. These may be considered under the three headings of shaping the political-military environment, warfighting, and deterrence.

USAF Role in Shaping the Political-Military Environment

The main shaping role for the U.S. armed forces is to prepare for possible combat with a potentially hostile China. However, as part of a policy of engagement, the USAF, as well as the rest of U.S. armed forces, have a role in conducting military-to-military contacts with the PLA.

First, such contacts can help shape China's strategic perceptions. Specifically, by demonstrating the gaps that exist between the PLA's capabilities and those of the U.S. armed forces, contacts may help curb any tendencies toward military adventurism that might crop up from time to time in Beijing. Demonstrating the superior technology, training, and tactics of the USAF to the Chinese can have, we believe, a meaningful deterrent effect.

Secondly, such contacts could increase U.S. knowledge of the PLA: not just its equipment and technical competence, but its organizational style, its norms, and its patterns of thought and behavior. Better understanding of how the PLA operates and where it fits into the overall structure of Chinese national security decisionmaking would enrich and improve U.S. assessments of China's strategic capabilities and intentions. *Contacts can serve this function, however, only if the United States is able to insist successfully on reciprocity* in the sense that the U.S. participants are able to gain significant insight into Chinese thinking and operations even as they afford the Chinese participants an opportunity to gain such insight with respect to the United States. Much greater effort must be made to fulfill this requirement on the U.S. side. This is something that can easily be overlooked, given the greater openness of U.S. society and the long Chinese tradition of keeping foreigners from learning too much about the way they operate; their strengths; and, especially, their weaknesses.

Finally, "military-to-military" contacts are really person-to-person contacts. Personal relationships between senior military leaders on both sides can provide a valuable informal conduit, a set of "back channels" that are useful from day to day and can prove vital in a time of crisis. In addition, such contacts can also help China better understand U.S. intentions.

Military-to-military contacts could take a wide variety of forms, including

- Air War College faculty and student exchange programs
- combined exercises for humanitarian missions
- Sino-U.S. conferences on regional military issues.

Warfighting Implications

Chinese military modernization poses many potential tasks for the U.S. armed forces, and the USAF in particular, as they seek to maintain a margin of military superiority over China. Among the most important implications for USAF are

- deployment and basing
- dealing with Chinese nuclear, biological, and chemical (NBC) weapons and missiles
- assuring air superiority
- confronting a spacefaring nation
- ensuring access to the theater.

Deployment and Basing. The future PLA may have substantial ability to interdict the flow of U.S. forces into East Asia in the event of a conflict between China and the United States. Sealift could be especially at risk. Ship movements could be tracked using radar-imaging satellites or long-range surveillance aircraft, both of which appear to be high priorities for acquisition or development. Attacks could be prosecuted by submarines (as noted earlier, the PLAN is building a new diesel submarine, buying a second kind, and developing a new SSN) employing advanced antiship missiles and/or modern torpedoes. A successful attack on even a single U.S. transport vessel would not only have serious operational implications—would the U.S. Navy need to disrupt its power-projection operations to help convoy sealift into the theater?—but could constitute a strategic event that

undermines U.S. political support. The USAF could find itself helping to protect sealift, either directly—for example, by providing additional sea surveillance or conducting operations to restrict Chinese
reconnaissance—or indirectly, by carrying more of the burden of
theater operations to free U.S. naval assets for escort tasks.

The USAF will face increased challenges to its deployment and basing plans, as well. By 2015, the Chinese could field hundreds of accurate, conventionally armed surface-to-surface cruise and ballistic
missiles. These weapons will be able to hit virtually any important
U.S. base in the theater, from Osan to Misawa, Kadena, and Guam.
High-value aircraft, such as the U.S. Airborne Warning and Control
System, tankers, Joint Surveillance and Target Attack Radar Systems,
and strategic airlifters, will be especially vulnerable, because they
must be parked in the open. An operational style that depends on
being able to pack such assets cheek by jowl on all available tarmac,
such as was often seen in the 1991 Gulf War, will be wholly untenable
when those aprons can literally be blanketed with plane-killing submunitions.[10]

China's ability to attack air bases successfully will also complicate
U.S. deployment planning. The Civil Reserve Air Fleet (CRAF) is a
vital component of U.S. air mobility, and no major deployment can
be accomplished without some level of CRAF participation. The contractual arrangement between the Department of Defense and the
airlines, however, puts very strict limitations on CRAF's employment
under combat conditions. Put simply, it may not be possible to
operate CRAF jets into or out of bases that are under attack or persistent threat of attack. If this proves to be the case, U.S. airlift into the
Western Pacific could be severely reduced in a scenario of Sino-U.S.
conflict.[11]

---

[10]For a detailed discussion of the numbers and characteristics of weapons needed to
devastate any array of aircraft parked in the open, see Stillion and Orletsky (1999).

[11]Even if the airlines are not contractually obligated to allow their aircraft to operate
into a "hot" base, it is entirely possible that a scheme of indemnification could be
arranged to permit at least some CRAF operations. CRAF could instead be used to
move men and equipment to a "safe" base where they could be transloaded onto
USAF aircraft for delivery into the theater itself. In either case, there would almost
certainly be a negative impact on deployment—in the first, because the necessary
negotiations would not occur instantaneously, thereby delaying movement; in the

USAF combat operations could also be jeopardized by attacks on bases. Even assuming that combat aircraft are protected in hardened shelters, personnel quarters will typically be vulnerable to attack, as will many maintenance and air-traffic control facilities. Fuel storage and distribution points could also be tempting targets for sufficiently accurate missiles.

Dealing with Chinese NBC Weapons and Missiles. Prudence requires taking into account the possibility that, in the future, China's missiles could also be tipped with NBC payloads, creating even more difficulties for U.S. operations. Although the USAF trains its personnel to work in a chemically contaminated environment, the direct effects of chemical attacks on sortie generation do not appear to be well understood and could be considerable.[12]

The indirect effects of such attacks could be even more devastating. For example, U.S. deployment could be severely curtailed if allies in the region refused to allow chemically contaminated transport aircraft to stage through bases on their territory.[13] In general, the problem of how such weapons would affect allied willingness to cooperate with us is difficult to answer; in particular, it could be that the mere *threat* of Chinese use of such weapons would limit our access to bases, ports, etc. In addition, unloading at sea ports of debarkation depends on hundreds if not thousands of civilian personnel—dock workers, machinery operators, truck drivers, and so on. It seems possible—indeed probable—that even a small chemical attack on a port could induce a large portion of these critical employees to absent themselves from work, greatly slowing the movement of equipment off ships and into action. To the extent that munitions are sealifted into the theater, either from bases ashore or on prepositioning vessels, the USAF would find itself hampered by any such reductions in throughput.

We believe the threat of persistent, large-scale NBC attack on bases and other key rear-area targets represents one of the largest chal-

---

second, because of simple inefficiencies resulting from the need to move the cargo from one aircraft to another.

[12]See, for example, Chow et al. (1998).

[13]Indeed, limited ability to decontaminate large aircraft appears to be one of the major difficulties that the USAF would confront in an NBC environment.

lenges the USAF will face in the next decade or two. It is unclear to what extent an explicit or implied threat of nuclear retaliation would be sufficient to deter Chinese use of chemical or biological weapons, or even of nuclear weapons against deployed forces in circumstances under which collateral civilian damage could be minimized. While defenses against ballistic and cruise missiles and countermeasures against chemical and biological warfare agents constitute key elements in coping with the threat (assuming the Chinese are not deterred), other means must be considered as well. These could include

- an increased emphasis on longer-range platforms that could be based outside the range of most future attack systems

- new operational concepts for forward operations that dramatically reduce the number of personnel and amount of equipment put at risk in the theater

- a more diversified basing infrastructure that allows USAF operations to be distributed across a larger number of installations, hence forcing the adversary to spread its attacks more thinly.[14]

Assuring Air Superiority. Unlike Iraq in 1991 or North Korea today, a modernized Chinese military could mount a sustained challenge to U.S. supremacy in the air. While the USAF will retain a broad qualitative advantage, the PLAAF will likely field enough advanced fighters—probably equipped with sophisticated AMRAAM-like "fire-and-forget" missiles and supported by airborne early warning platforms—to contest immediate U.S. dominance in the air-to-air arena. Large numbers of advanced SAMs—SA-10, HQ-9, SA-15, and others—will pose a difficult defense-suppression problem. Mobile and arrayed in mutually supporting layers, these systems will demand a great deal of attention; many sorties and high-quality munitions will be needed to neutralize them.[15]

---

[14]While increasing the number of bases can only help, if the total number were still small, this would be of only limited value.

[15]The early days of a conflict with China could be an extremely stressful period for the USAF. Consider a situation in which deployment is slowed by attacks on sealift and missile strikes on bases and ports. The forces that can make it into the theater could be subjected to chemical and biological warfare attacks, reducing their sortie rates, and will still have to cope with multiple competing demands, including suppression of

Two points seem worth emphasizing in this context. First, the USAF should continue to field aircraft and munitions with appreciable low-observable "stealth" characteristics. Future Chinese fighter pilots and SAM operators will be capable of killing targets they can locate and track. Shrinking their engagement envelopes by reducing their effective detection ranges will be an important factor in gaining and maintaining air superiority.

Second, the USAF should reevaluate the quantities of next-generation munitions it intends to buy because planned numbers may be insufficient to wage an effective campaign against a modernized PLA. The defense-suppression campaign alone could consume an enormous number of Joint Standoff Weapons and Joint Air-to-Surface Standoff Missiles in killing mobile SA-10s and HQ-9s. Other high-priority targets, such as bridges, command-and-control centers, and mobile missile launchers, will also need to be engaged even while defense-suppression operations are in full swing; accomplishing this will require numerous precise standoff weapons. Finally, the high-threat air-defense environment will make multiple passes or reattack missions very unappealing; an adequate stockpile of modern munitions can do much to minimize the need for such dangerous tactics.

Confronting a Spacefaring Nation. The 1991 Gulf War demonstrated, among other things, what can happen when a nation that does not enjoy the benefits of space exploitation wages war against one that does. In that conflict, the United States enjoyed a virtual monopoly on access to space-based surveillance, communications, and navigation support. This situation is unlikely to be repeated in the future, as capabilities that were once the sole domain of a superpower—such as high-resolution imagery—become available commercially and as more and more nations mount indigenous space programs.

As we discussed earlier, China—a relatively wealthy and technologically sophisticated power—is likely to reap significant benefits from space exploitation. The PLA's access to a wide range of space-based capabilities, both indigenous and foreign, military and commercial,

---

enemy air defenses, offensive and defensive air-to-air operations, countermissile strikes, and attacks against enemy naval and ground forces. Clearly a full plate for any future Joint Forces Air Component Commander.

will have important ramifications for the United States in the event of a crisis or conflict with China.

Space-based surveillance and remote sensing will greatly increase the PLA's situational awareness. The precise beddown of USAF assets, for example, will probably be known to Chinese leaders with sufficient timeliness and detail to permit effective targeting for missile and air attacks. Redundant satellite communication links, no doubt including some utilizing multinational or commercial assets, will make the PLA's command-and-control system more robust and difficult to disable.[16] Chinese forces will exploit GPS, GLONASS, and perhaps China's own planned *Twin Star* system for precise navigation and guidance. The PLA will, in other words, have access to space capabilities broadly similar to many of those that served U.S. forces so well in Desert Storm. And because much of this will flow from assets China does not own, the United States may find it difficult to restrict Beijing's access to it.

The U.S. military space constellation, however, could be a very lucrative target for attack. China's possible interest in a variety of antisatellite capabilities, ranging from jammers and blinders to directed-energy weapons, has already been noted. In a fight with China, the USAF would need to consider seriously how to protect its own space assets from attack and/or interference. While an ability to neutralize China's own space capabilities may offer some measure of deterrence, U.S. planners should at least consider the possibility that the Chinese—perceiving themselves to be far less dependent on space than the ultra-high-tech U.S. military—would consider a mutually blinding counterspace campaign to redound significantly to Beijing's benefit.

Ensuring Access to the Theater. The current U.S. basing posture in the Western Pacific is something of a Cold War legacy, oriented toward North Korea and the Pacific regions of the old Soviet Union. A crisis with China, however, could occur virtually anywhere in the region, from the vicinity of Southeast Asia north to Taiwan and then on to northeast Asia. Existing bases are not particularly well situated to support a U.S. response across this broad expanse; they offer little

---

[16]It is even conceivable that both the Chinese and U.S. militaries will be leasing different transponders on the same commercial satellites.

in the way of access to support Taiwan and virtually nothing in the South China Sea.

Looking to the future, Korean unification—or reconciliation short of unification that nonetheless removes the risk of conflict between Pyongyang and Seoul—could further reduce U.S. basing options in the area. A dramatic easing or elimination of tensions on the Korean peninsula could be followed by a drawdown in U.S. forces stationed there and a reduction or even elimination of American access to Korean bases. U.S. access to bases in Japan could also be cut back in the wake of positive events in Korea.

Long-range aircraft, such as heavy bombers, can help ease some of the problems incurred by an inadequate basing structure. However, the current bomber fleet may not be capable of generating sufficient sorties to provide the kind of operational tempo and mass required, especially in the early days of a contingency. Too, heavy bombers require support not just from tankers but from short-range fighters and defense-suppression assets that must be based somewhere. Clearly, they are not a complete and total solution. A medium bomber requiring fewer supporting assets might be an attractive solution.[17]

The USAF, then, needs to consider options for improving its access to the Western Pacific. In the near term, we suggest that the Air Force build on its successful history of exercises and joint training with friendly nations in Southeast Asia and Australasia to gain agreements and develop infrastructure to support expeditionary deployments in that area. Thailand, Singapore, Malaysia, Australia, New Zealand, Indonesia, the Philippines, and perhaps even Vietnam are potential candidates for more robust access accords.

In the longer term, the USAF should work to ensure continued access to Japanese and Korean bases independent of the state of relations between the two Koreas. Also, the USAF should consider whether longer range might not be a desirable characteristic in its next generation of combat aircraft.

---

[17]Stillion and Orletsky (1999) discusses such a bomber.

DETERRENCE IMPLICATIONS

Obviously, the U.S. armed forces have a role in deterring China from any future hostile action. Most of the requirements for this have been discussed in the warfighting section. To the extent that it can be made evident that U.S. forces can deny China the ability to achieve its goals by military means, deterrence will be that much stronger. To what extent the U.S. explicitly refers to deterrence of China as a mission of its armed forces would depend on the overall policy adopted; in any case, the general deterrent effect of U.S. military power will make itself felt in the region regardless of how explicit U.S. policy statements are about it. Nevertheless, the question arises whether deterrence of China poses any special difficulties.

Need to Threaten High Levels of Violence

In several important instances in the past 50 years, the United States (or the Soviet Union) had to threaten high levels of violence to deter China, even when it was by far the weaker party. The United States hinted strongly at the possibility of using nuclear weapons to end the Chinese harassment of the off-shore islands of Jinmen (Quemoy) and Mazu (Matsu) in 1955;[18] similarly, the Soviets resorted to nuclear threats to end the series of border clashes initiated by China in March, 1969, and to force China to the bargaining table.

If this pattern is repeated in the future, it would imply that, along with maintaining its current nuclear superiority, the United States should consider whether some sort of strategic defense might be necessary to sustain the credibility of not only any future nuclear threat to China but also any threat of conventional homeland attacks.

---

[18]For example, President Eisenhower, when asked at a press conference on March 16, 1955, whether the United States would "use tactical atomic weapons in a general war in Asia?" responded that, "[a]gainst a strictly military target, I replied, the answer would be 'yes.'" Eisenhower "hoped this answer would have some effect in persuading the Chinese Communists of the strength of our determination." (Eisenhower, 1963, p. 477.)

Characteristics of the Chinese Use of Force

In the past, the PRC has tended to emphasize surprise in its use of force and has often tailored uses of force to achieve major psychological shock effects relative to the actual amount of force used. The goal is to create a *fait accompli* before the adversary is able to bring major forces to bear in the conflict area. China has used force deliberately to heighten tension in a region, believing that this will produce certain benefits for it (e.g., creation of difficulties in the adversary coalition, causing domestic political problems for the adversary).

This type of behavior may be difficult to deter. Threats to use limited amounts of force in reply may indeed play into the Chinese strategy: If the object is to create tension, the adversary's counterthreats help rather than hurt, as long as the harm they threaten to cause remains within acceptable bounds. The key notion here seems to be the question of controlling the level of tension and the risk of escalation rather than avoiding it altogether. Hence, in dealing with China, a strategy of carefully controlled escalatory threats and actions may be an inappropriate means of achieving a deterrent effect.

Instead, the U.S. armed forces must be able to demonstrate an ability to operate in the region so as to counteract the political effect the Chinese are trying to produce. For example, U.S. willingness to deploy two carrier battle groups near Taiwan during the 1996 crisis played an important role in countering the psychological effect of the Chinese military exercises. Preserving the capability to bring airpower to bear close to Taiwan (or any other locus of a potential Chinese use of force), whether from carriers, by means of expeditionary forces, or from more distant bases, will be an important military prerequisite of a strong deterrence posture.

CONCLUSION

China is in the midst of one of the most remarkable processes of economic growth and modernization that the world has ever seen. If it is not derailed by the current Asian financial crisis or some other domestic or international crisis in the future, China could achieve a GNP roughly equal to that of the United States within the next several decades.

This of course would not mean that China was the equal of the United States in economic or technological terms or that it had the ability to become a military equal. For one thing, China's much larger population would mean that its GNP per capita would be much lower than that of the United States; in case of an all-out mobilization, the United States would be able to divert a larger share of its GNP to defense.[19] More importantly, the United States would still maintain important technological superiority in almost all areas relevant to military power. Finally, the military "capital" of the United States, in both hardware and software terms, would be much greater than that of China.

Nevertheless, such a China could develop the military capability to pose important challenges to the United States, especially in the East Asian region. Aside from the obvious flash point—Taiwan—China could challenge U.S. influence in the region and could seek to limit U.S. military and perhaps economic access. As long as China retains its current political system, it is likely to see the United States as an ideological threat; this would be especially true if the United States emphasizes democracy and human rights in its foreign policy. However, the fundamental problem is in the anomalous condition of a Chinese regime that is seeking to maintain a communist political system while opening up to the rest of the world and affording its citizens at least economic freedom. Thus, a certain official Chinese suspiciousness of the United States seems inevitable.

Beyond that, one has to consider the typical tendency of a "rising power" to challenge the existing predominant power, in this case made somewhat more pointed by the sense that China, after more than a century of "national humiliation," is finally coming into its own and securing its rightful status in the world. Whether or not China eventually aims at becoming a global rival of the United States, it may believe that it is entitled to a "sphere of influence" in its region that would be incompatible with U.S. military presence and with U.S. alliances with Japan, South Korea, and other states in the area.

---

[19]Of course, under more normal circumstances (i.e., when the defense burden varies anywhere between 3 percent and, say, 10 percent), China would have no difficulty in matching U.S. defense spending dollar for dollar. At what point China would no longer be able to match U.S. defense spending is hard to say.

Of course, none of this is inevitable. Even after it achieves GNP parity with the United States, China could still feel that it had to concentrate its energies on internal development, and that task could take up most of the next century. China could well conclude that its national security interests would be better served by cooperation with the United States than by confrontation. Finally, China could evolve politically in such a way that it no longer felt threatened by U.S. ideological influence, perhaps because it had itself democratized, or had found some other solid basis of political legitimacy to replace Marxism. If such a China became focused primarily on domestic concerns, it might be able to achieve a voluntary reunification with Taiwan and might have no trouble accepting an indefinite U.S. military presence in the region.

Faced with these tremendous uncertainties, U.S. policy must be able to encourage the good outcomes while hedging against the unfavorable ones. The U.S. armed forces must play a large role in this process, both in terms of maintaining and expanding the military-to-military contacts that can support better relations and in understanding and preparing for the types of military challenges that China might pose several decades from now.

The geography of the East Asian region is much different from that of Western Europe and Northeast Asia, where so much of the attention of the U.S. military has been focused. Instead of defending a land frontier, the U.S. armed forces may be called upon to operate across a vast maritime theater, with widely spaced islands and littoral countries. USAF may require much more-flexible basing arrangements; longer-legged air-breathing systems; a greater ability to operate from space; and an ability to defend against, and operate within range of, ballistic and cruise missiles armed with conventional and unconventional warheads. In addition, it may be necessary to operate much more closely with the Navy, supplying the longer-legged bomber, reconnaissance, tanker, and other support platforms, while the shorter-legged fighters operate from carrier decks. These types of changes take decades to understand, to say nothing of the time involved in developing and procuring the new weapon systems they demand.

Although its development over the past two decades has been unprecedentedly rapid, China started from a very backward situation and still has a long way to go. The United States and its armed forces have adequate time to plan for the emergence of a possibly ambitious and resentful China on the world scene.

BIBLIOGRAPHY

ACDA—*see* U.S. Arms Control and Disarmament Agency.

"Accomplishing the Great Cause of the Reunification of the Motherland is the Common Wish of All Chinese People," *Xinhua* Domestic Service (in Chinese), Beijing, 0922 GMT January 30, 1996, in FBIS-CHI-96-021, 1996.

Allen, Kenneth W., Glenn Krumel, and Jonathan D. Pollack, *China's Air Force Enters the 21st Century*, Santa Monica, Calif.: RAND, MR-580-AF, 1995.

Anselmo, Joseph, "U.S. Eyes China Missile Threat," *Aviation Week & Space Technology*, Vol. 145, No. 21, October 21, 1996.

Armey, Richard, quoted in Marc Sandalow, "China Expected to Keep U.S. Trade Privileges," *San Francisco Chronicle*, June 24, 1997. Available at http://www.sfgate.com/cgi-bin/article.cgi?file=/chronicle/archive/1997/06/24/MN74637.DTL (last accessed May 11, 1999).

Austin, Greg, "The Strategic Implications of China's Public Order Crisis," *Survival*, Vol. 37, No. 2, Summer 1995.

_____, *China's Ocean Frontier: International Law, Military Force and National Development*, St. Leonards, NSW Australia: Allen & Unwin, 1998.

Bachman, David, "Domestic Sources of Chinese Foreign Policy," in Samuel Kim, ed., *China and the World: Chinese Foreign Relations in the Post–Cold War Era*, Boulder, Colo.: Westview Press, 1994.

Baker, James A., III, "The United States and Other Great Asian Powers," *Vital Speeches of the Day*, speech given on February 9, 1996, p. 391.

Baker, Nicola, and Leonard C. Sebastian, "The Problem with Parachuting: Strategic Studies and Security in the Asia/Pacific Region," *Journal of Strategic Studies*, Vol. 18, No. 3, September 1995.

Ball, Desmond, "Strategic Culture in the Asia-Pacific Region," *Security Studies*, Vol. 3, No. 1, Autumn 1993.

Barfield, Thomas J., *The Perilous Frontier: Nomadic Empires and China*, Cambridge, Mass.: Blackwell Publishers, Inc., 1989.

Barnett, A. Doak, *China and the Major Powers in East Asia*, Washington, D.C., The Brookings Institution, 1977.

_____, *The Making of Foreign Policy in China: Structure and Process*, Boulder, Colo.: Westview Press, 1985.

Barnett, Correlli, *The Collapse of British Power*, New York: William Morrow, 1972.

Barraclough, Geoffrey, ed., *The Times Atlas of World History*, London: Times Books, 1993.

Bartlett, Beatrice, *Monarchs and Ministers*, Berkeley, Calif.: University of California Press, 1991.

Baum, Julian, "No Refuge," *Far Eastern Economic Review*, 16 February 1995.

"Beijing Builds Su-27 Fighters from Russian Kits," *Jane's Defence Weekly*, June 10, 1998, p. 2.

Bernstein, Richard, and Ross H. Munro, "The Coming Conflict with China," *Foreign Affairs*, March/April 1997.

Bitzinger, Richard, "China's Defense Budget," *International Defense Review*, February 1995.

Blank, S., "Russia's Clearance Sale," *Jane's Intelligence Review*, November 1997, p. 520.

Bowen, Wyn, and Stanley Shepard, "Living Under the Red Missile Threat," *Jane's Intelligence Review*, December 1996, p. 561.

Brown, Lester, *Who Will Feed China?* New York: Norton, 1995.

Burles, Mark, *Chinese Policy Toward Russia and the Central Asian Republics*, Santa Monica, Calif.: RAND, MR-1045-AF, 1999.

Buzan, Barry, and Gerald Segal, "The Rise of Elite Powers: A Strategy for the Postmodern States," *World Policy Review*, Vol. 13, No. 3, Fall 1996.

Caldwell, John, and Alexander T. Lennon, "China's Nuclear Modernization Program," *Strategic Review*, Fall 1995.

"Can a Bear Love a Dragon?" *The Economist*, April 26, 1997.

Catley, Bob, and Makmur Keliat, *Spratlys: The Dispute in the South China Sea*, Aldershot, UK: Ashgate Publishing, 1997.

Chang, Gordon H., "To the Nuclear Brink: Eisenhower, Dulles, and the Quemoy-Matsu Crisis," *International Security*, Vol. 12, No. 4, Spring 1988.

Chen, K., "China's Inability to Keep Subs Running Shows Broader Woes Plaguing Military," *The Wall Street Journal*, August 1, 1997, p. A11.

Chen, King C., *Vietnam and China, 1938–1954*, Princeton, N.J.: Princeton University Press, 1969.

Chen Qimao, "New Approaches in China's Foreign Policy: The Post–Cold War Era," *Asian Survey*, Vol. 33, No. 3, March 1993.

"China and India are Expected to Become . . . ," *Aviation Week & Space Technology*, August 25, 1997, p. 17.

"China Calls for Concrete Measures to Implement Convention on Chemical Weapons," *Xinhua* News Agency, July 24, 1996.

"China Charts New Waters with Air-Capable Ship," *Jane's Defence Weekly*, June 10, 1998.

"China, France Sign Joint Declaration," *Beijing Review*, June 2–8, 1997.

"China Should Receive Its Third 'Kilo' by November," *Jane's Defence Weekly*, July 30, 1997, p. 16.

China Statistical Publishing House, *China Statistical Yearbook*, Beijing, 1998.

"Chinese 'GPS' Project Set," *Aviation Week & Space Technology*, October 17, 1994.

Chow, Brian, Greg Jones, Irving Lachow, John Stillion, Dean A. Wilkening, and Howell Yee, *Air Force Operations in a Chemical and Biological Environment*, Santa Monica, Calif.: RAND, DB-189/1-AF, 1998.

Christensen, Thomas J., "Threats, Assurances, and the Last Chance for Peace: The Lessons of Mao's Korean War Telegrams," *International Security*, Vol. 17, No. 1, Summer 1992.

_____, "Chinese Realpolitik," *Foreign Affairs*, Vol. 75, No. 5, September/October 1996a.

_____, *Useful Adversaries: Grand Strategy, Domestic Mobilization, and Sino-American Conflict, 1947–1958*, Princeton, N.J.: Princeton University Press, 1996b.

Chu Shulong, "Sino-U.S. Relations: The Necessity for Change and a New Strategy," *Contemporary International Relations*, English ed., Vol. 6, No. 11, November 1996.

Chun, Yen, "Unmasking the Secrets of Communist China's 'Nuclear Counterattack' Force," *Kuang Chiao Ching*, No. 282, March 16, 1996, in FBIS-CHI, March 16, 1996.

Clarke, Christopher M., "China's Transition to the Post-Deng Era," in *China's Economic Dilemmas in the 1990's: The Problems of Reforms, Modernization, and Interdependence*, study papers submitted to the Joint Economic Committee, Congress of the United States, Washington, D.C.: U.S. Government Printing Office, 1991.

"Clinton and Jiang in Their Own Words: Sharing a Broad Agenda," excerpts from a joint news conference with President Clinton and President Jiang, *New York Times*, October 30, 1997, pp. A20ff.

"Clinton: Extend China's Favored Trade Status," CNN Time All Politics, May 19, 1997. Article available at http://allpolitics.com/1997/05/19/china.mfn/ (last accessed April 30 1999).

Cohen, Eliot A., and John Gooch, *Military Misfortunes: The Anatomy of Failure in War*, New York: Vintage Books, 1991.

Cohen, Joel E., *How Many People Can the Earth Support?* New York: Norton, 1995.

Cohen, Paul A., "Ch'ing China: Confrontation with the West," *Modern East Asia: Essays in Interpretation*, New York: Harcourt, Brace & World, 1970.

Dai Xiaohua, "Why and How the U.S. Media Work to Demonize China," *Beijing Review*, Vol. 40, No. 31, August 4–10, 1997.

Davis, Zachary S., "China's Nonproliferation and Export Control Policies," *Asian Survey*, Vol. XXXV, No. 6, June 1995.

Dittmer, Lowell, "Bases of Power in Chinese Politics: A Theory and an Analysis of the Fall of the 'Gang of Four,'" *World Politics*, Vol. 31, No. 1, October 1978.

Dittmer, Lowell, and Samuel S. Kim, eds., *China's Quest for National Identity*, Ithaca, N.Y.: Cornell University Press, 1993.

Dong Guozheng, "Hegemonist Ambition Is Completely Exposed," *Jiefangjun Bao* [PLA Daily], May 19, 1998, p. 5, in FBIS-CHI-98-140, 1998.

Dorn, James A., "Trade and Human Rights in China," Cato Institute, November 15, 1996. Available at http://www.cato.org/dailys/11-15-96.html (last accessed April 30, 1999).

Doyle, Michael, "Kant, Liberal Legacies and Foreign Affairs, Part I," *Philosophy and Public Affairs*, Vol. 12, No. 3, Summer 1983.

Dreyer, Edward L., *Early Ming China*, Stanford, Calif.: Stanford University Press, 1982.

Dreyer, June Teufel, and Ilpyong, J. Kim, eds., *Chinese Defense and Foreign Policy*, New York: Paragon House, 1988.

The Economist Intelligence Unit, *Country Report: China, Mongolia*, London, 1999.

Eisenhower, Dwight D., *Mandate for Change: 1953–56*, Garden City, N.Y.: Doubleday & Company, Inc., 1963.

Ellings, Richard J., and Sheldon W. Simon, eds., *Southeast Asian Security in the New Millennium*, Armonk, N.Y.: M.E. Sharpe, 1996.

"Excerpts from White Paper on China's Arms Control and Disarmament," *Xinhua* News Agency, November 16, 1995.

Fairbank, John King, *China, A New History*, Cambridge, Mass.: Harvard University Press, 1992.

Fairbank, John King, ed., *The Chinese World Order*, Cambridge, Mass.: Harvard University Press, 1968.

Family Research Council, *Deconstructing 'Constructive Engagement': The Failure of US Policy Toward China*, Washington, D.C., 1997.

"The Grip Slips," *Far Eastern Economic Review*, May 11, 1995, pp. 18ff.

"Testing the Waters," *Far Eastern Economic Review*, March 12, 1992.

Farber, Henry S., and Joanne Gowa, "Politics and Peace," *International Security*, Vol. 20, No. 2, Fall 1995.

Fong Tak-ho and Michelle Lee, "Beijing Expected to Strengthen Military Against Taiwan, *Standard* (Hong Kong), March 2, 1999, p. 6, in FBIS-CHI-1999-0302, 1999.

Forbes, Andrew D. W., *Warlords and Muslims in Chinese Central Asia*, Cambridge, UK: Cambridge University Press, 1986.

Foreign Broadcast Information Service, "Russia: Increasing Arms Sales to PRC Viewed," October 5, 1996.

Freeman, Chas. W., Jr., "Managing U.S. Relations with China," presented at Asia/Pacific Research Center, Stanford University, April 1996.

_____, *Arts of Power: Statecraft and Diplomacy*, Washington, D.C.: U.S. Institute of Peace Press, 1997.

Friedberg, Aaron L., "Ripe for Rivalry: Prospects for Peace in a Multipolar Asia," *International Security*, Vol. 18, No. 3, Winter 1993/94.

Friedman, Milton, *Capitalism and Freedom*, Chicago: University of Chicago Press, 1982.

Frost, Gerald P., and Irving Lachow, *Satellite Navigation-Aiding for Ballistic and Cruise Missiles*, Santa Monica, Calif.: RAND, RP-543, 1996.

Fulgham, D. A., "China Exploiting U.S. Patriot Secrets," *Aviation Week & Space Technology*, January 18, 1993a, p. 20.

_____, "Defense Dept. Confirms Patriot Technology Diverted," *Aviation Week & Space Technology*, February 1, 1993b, p. 26.

Garret, Banning, and Bonnie Glaser, "Chinese Apprehensions about Revitalization of the U.S.-Japan Alliance," *Asian Survey*, Vol. XXXVII, No. 4, April 1997.

Garver, John W., *Face Off: China, the United States, and Taiwan's Democratization*, Seattle, Wash.: University of Washington Press, 1997.

_____, "China as Number One," *The China Journal*, No. 39, January 1998.

Gelman, Harry, *The Soviet Far East Buildup and Soviet Risk-Taking Against China*, Santa Monica, Calif.: RAND, R-2943-AF, 1982.

George, Alexander L., and Richard Smoke, *Deterrence in American Foreign Policy: Theory and Practice*, New York: Columbia University Press, 1974.

Gerardi, G., and R. Fisher, Jr., "China's Missile Tests Show More Muscle," *Jane's Intelligence Review*, March 11, 1997.

Gertz, B., "China Adds 6 ICBMs to Arsenal," *The Washington Times*, July 21, 1998.

Gill, Bates, and Taeho Kim, *China's Arms Acquisitions from Abroad: A Quest for 'Superb and Secret Weapons,'* New York: Oxford University Press, 1995.

Gilpin, Robert, *War and Change in World Politics*, New York: Cambridge University Press, 1981.

_____, "The Theory of Hegemonic War," *Journal of Interdisciplinary History*, Vol. XVIII, No. 4, Spring 1988.

Gittings, John, *The World and China, 1922–1972*, New York: Harper & Row, 1974.

Glaser, Bonnie S., "China's Security Perceptions: Interests and Ambitions," *Asian Survey*, Vol. 33, No. 3, March 1993.

Godwin, Paul H. B., "Changing Concepts of Doctrine, Strategy, and Operations in the People's Liberation Army 1978–87," *China Quarterly*, No. 112, December 1987.

_____, "From Continent to Periphery: PLA Doctrine, Strategy, and Capabilities Towards 2000," *China Quarterly*, No. 146, June 1996.

Goldstein, Avery, "Great Expectations: Interpreting China's Arrival," *International Security*, Vol. 22, No. 3, Winter 1997/98.

_____, "Robust and Affordable Security: Some Lessons from the Second-Ranking Powers During the Cold War," *Journal of Strategic Studies*, Vol. 15, No. 4, December 1992.

Goldstone, Jack A., "The Coming Chinese Collapse," *Foreign Policy*, Summer 1995.

Gompert, David C., "Right Makes Might: Freedom and Power in the Information Age," in Zalmay Khalilzad and John White, eds., *Strategic Appraisal: The Changing Role of Information in Warfare*, Santa Monica, Calif.: RAND, MR-1016-AF, 1999, pp. 45–73.

Hamrin, Carol Lee, "Elite Politics and the Development of China's Foreign Relations," in Thomas W. Robinson and David Shambaugh, eds., *Chinese Foreign Policy: Theory and Practice*, Oxford: Clarendon Press, 1994.

_____, "The Party Leadership System," in Kenneth G. Lieberthal and David M. Lampton, eds., *Bureaucracy, Politics, and Decision Making in Post-Mao China*, Berkeley, Calif.: University of California Press, 1992.

_____, *China and the Challenge of the Future: Changing Political Patterns*, Boulder, Colo.: Westview Press, 1990.

Hao Yufan and Zhai Zhihai, "China's Decision to Enter the Korean War," *China Quarterly*, No. 121, March 1990.

Harding, Harry, *China's Second Revolution, Reform after Mao*, Washington, D.C.: The Brookings Institution, 1987.

_____, *A Fragile Relationship: The United States and China since 1972*, Washington, D.C.: The Brookings Institution, 1992.

_____, "'On the Four Great Relationships': The Prospects for China," *Survival*, Vol. 36, No. 2, Summer 1994.

Harris, Stuart, and Gary Klintworth, eds., *China as a Great Power, Myths, Realities and Challenges in the Asia-Pacific Region*, New York: St. Martin's Press, 1995.

He Di, "The Evolution of the People's Republic of China's Policy toward the Offshore Islands," in Warren I. Cohen and Akira Iriye, eds., *The Great Powers in East Asia, 1953–1960*, New York: Columbia University Press, 1990.

Hecker, Jayetta Z., Associate Director of National Security and International Affairs of the General Accounting Office, testimony before the Committee on Banking and Financial Services, July 29, 1996.

Heilbrunn, Jacob, "Christian Rights," *The New Republic*, July 7, 1997.

Hinton, Harold C., *Communist China in World Politics*, Boston: Houghton Mifflin, 1966.

_____, "Conflict on the Ussuri: A Clash of Nationalism," *Problems of Communism*, January–April 1971.

Holloway, Nigel, "Jolt From the Blue," *Far Eastern Economic Review*, August 3, 1995.

Hong Kong Standard, "Jiang Issues Campus Gag Order on Diaoyu Islands," September 17, 1996.

Hu Weixing, "Beijing's New Thinking on Security Strategy," *The Journal of Contemporary China*, No. 3, Summer 1993.

Huang, Ray, *China: A Macro History*, New York: M. E. Sharpe, Inc., 1997.

Hucker, Charles O., *China to 1850: A Short History*, Stanford, Calif.: Stanford University Press, 1975.

Hunt, Michael H., "Chinese National Identity and the Strong State: The Late Qing-Republican Crisis," in Lowell Dittmer and Samuel S. Kim, eds., *China's Quest for National Identity*, Ithaca, N.Y.: Cornell University Press, 1993.

_____, *The Genesis of Chinese Communist Foreign Policy*, New York: Columbia University Press, 1996.

IISS—*see* International Institute for Strategic Studies.

Information Office of the State Council of the People's Republic of China, "China: Arms Control and Disarmament," November 1995, in *Beijing Review*, November 27–December 3, 1995.

International Institute for Strategic Studies, *The Military Balance 1998/99*, London: Oxford University Press, October 1998.

Isby, D. C., *Weapons and Tactics of the Soviet Army*, rev. ed., London: Jane's, 1988.

Jervis, Robert, "Deterrence Theory Revisited," *World Politics*, Vol. 31, No. 2, January 1979.

Jian, Chen, *China's Road to the Korean War: The Making of the Sino-American Confrontation*, New York: Columbia University Press, 1994.

Jiang Zemin, Speech, 30 January 1995, "Continue to Promote the Reunification of the Motherland," as reported by Xinhua (in English), Beijing, 0618 GMT 30 January 1995, in FBIS-CHI-95-019, 1995.

Joffe, Ellis, "Party-Army Relations in China: Retrospect and Prospect," *China Quarterly*, No. 146, June 1996, pp. 299–314.

Johnson, Lyndon B., *The Vantage Point: Perspectives of the Presidency, 1963–69*, New York: Holt, Rinehart and Winston, 1971.

Johnston, Alastair Iain, *Cultural Realism: Strategic Culture and Grand Strategy in Chinese History*, Princeton, N.J.: Princeton University Press, 1995.

"Joint Statement by Chinese and US Heads of State on the South Asian Issue, 27 June 1998, Beijing," Xinhua Domestic Service (in Chinese), Beijing, 1249 GMT June 27, 1998, translated in FBIS-CHI-98-178, 1998.

"Joint Statement by the People's Republic of China and the Russian Federation on the Multipolarization of the World and the Establishment of a New International Order," *Beijing Review*, May 12–18, 1997.

Jordan, J., "The People's Liberation Army Navy (PLAN)," *Jane's Intelligence Review*, June 1994.

Kaye, Lincoln, "The Grip Slips," *Far Eastern Economic Review*, May 11, 1995.

Keohane, Robert O., and Joseph S. Nye, Jr., "Power and Interdependence Revisited," *International Organization*, Autumn 1987.

Khong, Yuen Foong, *Analogies at War: Korea, Munich, Dien Bien Phu, and the Vietnam Decisions of 1965*, Princeton, N.J.: Princeton University Press, 1992.

Kim, Samuel S., ed., *China and the World: Chinese Foreign Relations in the Post–Cold War Era*, Boulder, Colo.: Westview Press, 1994.

_____, *China and the World: Chinese Foreign Policy in the Post-Mao Era*, Boulder, Colo.: Westview Press, 1984.

_____, *China and the World: Chinese Foreign Relations in the Post–Cold War Era*, Boulder, Colo.: Westview Press, 1984.

_____, "China as a Regional Power," *Current History*, Vol. 91, No. 566, September 1992.

Kissinger, Henry, *White House Years*, Boston: Little, Brown and Company, 1979.

Kirby, William C., "Traditions of Centrality, Authority, and Management of Modern China's Foreign Relations," in Thomas W.

Robinson and David Shambaugh, eds., *Chinese Foreign Policy: Theory and Practice*, Oxford: Clarendon Press, 1994.

Kristof, Nicholas, "The Rise of China," *Foreign Affairs*, Vol. 72, No. 5, November 1993.

Kupchan, Charles A., and Clifford A. Kupchan, "The Promise of Collective Security, *International Security*, Vol. 20, No. 1, Summer 1995.

Lackritz, Marc E., "Testimony before the House Committee on Banking and Financial Services," July 29, 1996.

Lampton, David M., *Paths to Power: Elite Mobility in Contemporary China*, Center for Chinese Studies, Ann Arbor: University of Michigan, 1989.

_____, "China Policy in Clinton's First Year," in James R. Lilley and Wendall Wilkie II, *Beyond MFN*, Washington, D.C.: AEI Press, 1994.

Lamson, J. A., and W. Q. Bowen, "'One Arrow, Three Stars': China's MIRV Programme, Part One," *Jane's Intelligence Review*, Vol. 9, No. 5.

Layne, Christopher, "Kant or Cant: The Myth of the Democratic Peace," *International Security*, Vol. 19, No. 2, Fall 1994.

Lardy, Nicholas R., "China's Growing Economic Role in Asia," in "The Future of China," *NBR Analysis*, Vol. 3, No. 3, August 1992.

Lavin, Franklin L., "Watching the Dragon," *National Review*, October 14, 1996.

Lee, Choon Kun, *War in the Confucian International Order*, Doctoral Dissertation, The University of Texas at Austin, August 1988.

"Legitimate Rights and the Interests of the Chinese in Indonesia Must Be Protected," *Renmin Ribao* (People's Daily), August 3, 1998, p. 1, translated in FBIS-CHI-98-218, 1998.

Lennox, Duncan, ed., *Jane's Strategic Weapon Systems*, Issue 18, May 1995.

Lennox, Duncan, and Barbara Starr, "Cruise Missiles," *Jane's Defence Weekly*, Vol. 25, No. 18, May 1, 1996, p. 19.

Lewis, J. W., and L. Xue, *China's Strategic Seapower*, Stanford, Calif.: Stanford University Press, 1994.

Li, Nan, "The PLA's Evolving Warfighting Doctrine, Strategy, and Tactics, 1985–95: A Chinese Perspective," *China Quarterly*, No. 146, June 1996.

Liang Liangxing, ed., *China's Foreign Relations: A Chronology of Events (1948–1988)*, Beijing: Foreign Languages Press, 1989.

Liao, Kuang-sheng, *Antiforeignism and Modernization in China, 1860–1980: Linkage Between Domestic Politics and Foreign Policy*, New York: St. Martin's Press, 1984.

_____, "Linkage Politics in China: Internal Mobilization and Articulated External Hostility in the Cultural Revolution, 1967–1969," *World Politics*, Vol. 28, No. 4, 1976.

Lieberthal, Kenneth, "A New China Strategy," *Foreign Affairs*, Vol. 74, No. 6, November/December 1995.

_____, "China in the Year 2000: Politics and International Security," in "The Future of China," *NBR Analysis*, Vol. 3, No. 3, August 1992.

_____, "Domestic Politics and Foreign Policy" in Harry Harding, ed., *China's Foreign Relations in the 1980s*, New Haven, Conn.: Yale University Press, 1984.

Lieberthal, Kenneth G., and Michael Lampton, eds., *Bureaucracy, Politics, and Decision Making in Post-Mao China*, Berkeley: University of California Press, 1992.

Lilley, James R., "Trade and the Waking Giant—China, Asia, and American Engagement," in James R. Lilley and Wendall Willkie II, *Beyond MFN*, Washington, D.C.: AEI Press, 1994.

Liu, Xuecheng, *The Sino-Indian Border Dispute and Sino-Indian Relations*, Lanham, Md.: University Press of America, 1994.

Luard, Evan, *The Blunted Sword: The Erosion of Military Power in Modern World Politics*, New York: New Amsterdam, 1988.

MacFarquhar, Roderick, and John K. Fairbank, eds., "The People's Republic, Part 2: Revolutions within the Chinese Revolution 1966–1982," in Denis Twitchett and John K. Fairbank, eds., *The Cambridge History of China*, Vol. 15, Cambridge, England: Cambridge University Press, 1991.

Malik, J. Mohan, "China-India Relations in the Post-Soviet Era: The Continuing Rivalry," *China Quarterly*, No. 142, June 1995.

Malik, J. Mohan, ed., *Asian Defence Policies*, Geelong, Victoria, Australia: Deakin University Press, 1993.

Mansfield, Edward D., and Jack Snyder, "Democratization and the Danger of War," *International Security*, Vol. 20, No. 1, Summer 1995.

Maxwell, Neville, *India's China War*, New York: Random House, 1970.

McNaugher, Thomas L., "A Strong China: Is the United States Ready?" *The Brookings Review*, Fall 1994.

Mearsheimer, John, "Back to the Future: Instability in Europe After the Cold War," *International Security*, Vol. 19, No. 3, Winter 1994/95.

Meyers, Steven Lee, "U.S. Asserting Iran Link, Bars 2 Chinese Firms," *New York Times*, May 22, 1997, p. A1.

Modelski, George, "The Long Cycle of Global Politics and the Nation-State," *Comparative Studies in Society and History*, April 1978.

Morganthau, Hans, *Politics Among Nations*, New York: Alfred K. Knopf, 1968.

Morrison, Wayne M., and John P. Hardt, "Sino-U.S. Economic Relations into the 21st Century," in *China's Economic Future: Challenges to U.S. Policy*, study papers submitted to the Joint Economic Committee, Congress of the United States, Washington: U.S. Government Printing Office, 1996.

Mueller, John, *Retreat from Doomsday: The Obsolescence of Major War*, New York: Basic Books, 1989.

Mulvenon, James, ed., *China Facts and Figures Annual Handbook 21*, Gulf Breeze, Fla.: Academic International Press, 1997.

Munro, Ross H., testimony prepared for the Senate Subcommittee on East Asian and Pacific Affairs, October 12, 1995.

Nathan, Andrew J., "Bull in the China Shop," *The New Republic*, August 12, 1996.

National Defense Panel, *Transforming Defense: National Security in the 21st Century*, Arlington, Va., 1997.

Novichkov, N., and M. A. Taverna, "Russia, Israel Plan A-50; Ukraine Signs Iran Deal," *Aviation Week & Space Technology*, June 23, 1997.

Nye, Joseph S., Jr., "The Case for Deep Engagement," *Foreign Affairs*, Vol. 74, No. 4, July/August 1995.

O'Neill, Hugh B., *Companion to Chinese History*, New York: Facts on File Publications, 1987.

Office of the Secretary of Defense, *Proliferation: Threat and Response*, Washington, D.C.: U.S. Government Printing Office, November, 1997.

Oksenberg, Michel, and Elizabeth Economy, *Shaping U.S.-China Relations*, New York: Council on Foreign Relations, 1997.

Oksenberg, Michel C., Michael D. Swaine, Daniel C. Lynch, "The Chinese Future," report prepared for Study Group by Pacific Council on International Policy and RAND Center for Asia-Pacific Policy, no date.

Organski, A. F. K., and Jacek Kugler, *The War Ledger*, Chicago: University of Chicago Press, 1980.

Orme, John, "The Utility of Force in a World of Scarcity," *International Security*, Vol. 22, No. 3, Winter 1997/98.

Paine, S. C. M., *Imperial Rivals: China, Russia, and Their Disputed Frontier*, New York: M. E. Sharpe, Inc., 1996.

Palit, D. K., *War in High Himalaya: The Indian Army in Crisis, 1962*, New York: St. Martin's Press, 1991.

Paltiel, Jeremy, "PLA Allegiance on Parade: Civil-Military Relations in Transition," *China Quarterly*, No. 143, September 1995, pp. 784–800.

Papayoanou, Paul A., "Interdependence, Institutions, and the Balance of Power: Britain, Germany, and World War I," *International Security*, Vol. 20, No. 4, Spring 1996.

Periscope, C801 Ying Ji 1 (Hawk Attack 1), July 1, 1998. Available at http://www.periscope.ucg.com/weapons/missrock/antiship/w0000660.html (last accessed May 27, 1999).

Polmar, N., *Guide to the Soviet Navy (4th edition)*, Annapolis, Md.: Naval Institute Press, 1986.

Pomfret, John, "Clinton Restates 'Three Noes' Policy on Taiwan," *Washington Post*, June 30, 1998.

Porteous, Holly, "China's View of Strategic Weapons," *Jane's Intelligence Review*, Vol. 8, No. 3, March 1996.

Pye, Lucian, "China: Erratic State, Frustrated Society," *Foreign Affairs*, Vol. 69, No. 4, Fall 1990.

_____, "How China's Nationalism Was Shanghaied," *Australian Journal of Chinese Affairs*, No. 29, January 1993.

Robinson, Thomas W., *The Sino-Soviet Border Dispute: Background, Development, and the March 1969 Clashes*, Santa Monica, Calif.: RAND, 1970.

Robinson, Thomas W., and David Shambaugh, eds., *Chinese Foreign Policy: Theory and Practice*, Oxford: Clarendon Press, 1994.

Rohwer, Jim, "Asia: A Billion Consumers," *The Economist*, October 30, 1993.

Ropelewski, Robert, and Pierre Condom, "US and Europe Compete for Share of China Growth," *Interavia*, October 1995.

Rosecrance, Richard N., *The Rise of the Trading State: Commerce and Conquest in the Modern World*, New York: Basic Books, 1986.

Ross, Robert S., *The Indochina Tangle: China's Vietnam Policy, 1975–1979*, New York: Columbia University Press, 1988.

Rossabi, Morris, ed., *China Among Equals*, Berkeley: University of California Press, 1983.

"Russia Helps China Take New SSNs Into Silent Era," *Jane's Defence Weekly*, August 13, 1997, 14..

SarDesai, D. R., *Vietnam: Past and Present*, Boulder, Colo.: Westview Press, 1998.

Schelling, Thomas C., *Arms and Influence*, New Haven, Conn.: Yale University Press, 1966.

Sciolino, Elaine, "The Schooling of Gingrich, the Foreign Policy Novice," *The New York Times*, July 18, 1995.

Segal, Gerald, *Defending China*, Oxford: Oxford University Press, 1985.

Segal, Gerald, and William T. Tow, eds., *Chinese Defence Policy*, Chicago: University of Illinois Press, 1984.

Shambaugh, David, "China's Security Strategy in Post–Cold War Era," *Survival*, Vol. 34, No. 2, Summer 1992.

_____, "Containment or Engagement of China? Calculating Beijing's Responses," *International Security*, Vol. 21, No. 2, Fall 1996.

_____, "Chinese Hegemony over East Asia by 2015?" *Korean Journal of Defense Analysis*, Vol. IX, No. 1, Summer 1997, pp. 7–28.

Shambaugh, David, and Richard H. Yang, eds., *China's Military in Transition*, Oxford: Clarendon Press, 1997.

Sharpe, R. (Capt., RN), ed., *Jane's Fighting Ships 1997–98*, London: Jane's Information Group, 1997.

Shinn, James, ed., *Weaving the Net: Conditional Engagement with China*, New York: Council on Foreign Relations, 1996.

Shirk, Susan, *The Political Logic of Economic Reform in China*, Berkeley: University of California Press, 1993.

Shlapak, D. A., and G. Jones, *The Dog That Won't Bark: The Chinese Military's Approach to Space Exploitation*, Santa Monica, Calif.: RAND, unpublished manuscript.

"Special Issue: China's Military in Transition," *China Quarterly*, No. 146, June 1996.

Spector, Leonard S., "Prepared Testimony of Leonard S. Spector, Nuclear Non-Proliferation Project, Carnegie Endowment for International Peace, Before the House International Relations Committee, Re: Consequences of China's Military Sales to Iran," *Federal News Service*, September 12, 1996.

Spence, Jonathan D., *The Search for Modern China*, New York: W. W. Norton & Company, 1990.

Spiro, David E., "The Insignificance of the Liberal Peace," *International Security*, Vol. 19, No. 2, Fall 1994.

Stillion, J., and D. Orletsky, *Airbase Vulnerability to Conventional Cruise-Missile and Ballistic-Missile Attacks: Technology, Scenarios, and U.S. Air Force Responses*, Santa Monica, Calif.: RAND, MR-1028-AF, 1999.

Stokes, M. A. (Maj.), *China's Strategic Modernization: Implications for U.S. National Security*, USAF Institute for National Security Studies, October 1997.

Sun Tzu, *The Art of War*, tr. Samuel B. Griffith, New York: Oxford University Press, 1963.

Sutter, Robert G., *East Asia: Disputed Islands and Offshore Claims— Issues for U.S. Policy*, Washington, D.C.: Congressional Research Service, Library of Congress, 92-614S, July 28, 1992.

Sutter, Robert G., Shirley Kan, and Kerry Dumbaugh, *China in Transition: Changing Conditions and Implications for U.S. Interests*, Washington, D.C.: Congressional Research Service, Library of Congress, December 20, 1993.

Swaine, Michael D., "Leadership Succession in China: Implications for Domestic and Regional Stability," paper prepared for the RAND-Sejong Project on East Asia's Potential for Instability and Crisis, February 1995.

_____, "China," in Zalmay Khalilzad, ed., *Strategic Appraisal 1996*, Santa Monica, Calif.: RAND, MR-543-AF, 1996, pp. 185–221.

_____, *China: Domestic Change and Foreign Policy*, Santa Monica, Calif.: RAND, MR-604-OSD, 1995.

Swaine, Michael D., and Ashley Tellis, *Interpreting China's Grand Strategy*, Santa Monica, Calif.: RAND, unpublished manuscript.

Swanson, Bruce, *Eighth Voyage of the Dragon: A History of China's Quest for Seapower*, Naval Institute Press, 1982.

Taylor, Keith W., "The Early Kingdoms," in Nicholas Tarling, ed., *The Cambridge History of Southeast Asia: From Early Times to C. 1800*, Cambridge, U.K.: Cambridge University Press, 1993, pp. 137–150.

Taylor, M. J. H., ed., *Jane's World Combat Aircraft*, Jane's Information Group, London, 1988.

Tellis, Ashley J., Chung Min Lee, James Mulvenon, Courtney Purrington, and Michael D. Swaine, "Sources of Conflict in Asia," in Zalmay Khalilzad and Ian O. Lesser, eds., *Sources of Conflict in the 21st Century: Regional Futures and U.S. Strategy*, Santa Monica, Calif.: RAND, MR-897-AF, 1998, pp. 43–170.

"'Text' of Beijing-Paris Declaration," *Xinhua* (in English), Beijing, 0905 GMT, May 16, 1997, FBIS-CHI-97-095, 1997.

Thompson, William R., ed., "Succession Crises in the Global Political System," in Albert L. Bergesen, *Crises in the World-System*, Beverly Hills: Sage Publications, 1983.

_____, "Uneven Economic Growth, Systemic Challenges and Global Wars," *International Studies Quarterly*, Vol. 27, No. 3, September 1983.

_____, *On Global War*, Columbia, S.C.: University of South Carolina Press, 1988.

Townsend, James, "Chinese Nationalism," *Australian Journal of Chinese Affairs*, January 1992.

Truesdell, Amy, "Cruise Missiles: The Discriminating Weapon of Choice?" *Jane's Intelligence Review*, Vol. 9, No. 2, February 1997, pp. 87–90.

Truman, Harry S, *Memoirs*, Vol. 2: *Years of Trial and Hope*, Garden City, N.Y.: Doubleday, 1956.

Tsou, Tang, *America's Failure in China, 1941–50*, Chicago: University of Chicago Press, 1963.

Tyler, Patrick E., "As China Threatens Taiwan, It Makes Sure U.S. Listens," *New York Times*, January 24, 1996.

U.S. Arms Control and Disarmament Agency, *Threat Control Through Arms Control: Annual Report to Congress 1995*, Washington, D.C.: U.S. Arms Control and Disarmament Agency, 1996.

_____, *World Military Expenditures and Arms Transfers 1996*, Washington, D.C.: U.S. Arms Control and Disarmament Agency, 1997.

U.S. Congress, *China's Economic Dilemmas in the 1990's: The Problems of Reforms, Modernization, and Interdependence*, Vol. 1, study papers submitted to the Joint Economic Committee, Washington, D.C.: U.S. Government Printing Office, 1991.

U.S. Department of Defense, *Selected Military Capabilities of the People's Republic of China*, Washington, D.C., no date.

_____, *United States Security Strategy for the East Asia-Pacific Region*, Washington, D.C., 1995.

United States Code Congressional and Administrative News: 96th Congress, First Session 1979, St. Paul, Minn.: West Publishing Company, 93 Stat. 14, 1979.

_____, St. Paul, Minn.: West Publishing Company, 93 Stat. 15, 1980.

Valencia, Mark J., *China and the South China Sea Disputes*, Adelphi Paper 298, Oxford: Oxford University Press, 1995.

Wakeman, Frederic, Jr., *Strangers at the Gate: Social Disorder in South China 1839–1861*, Berkeley: University of California Press, 1966.

Waldron, Arthur, *From War to Nationalism: China's Turning Point, 1924–1925*, Cambridge:, U.K.: Cambridge University Press, 1995.

_____, "How Not to Deal with China," *Commentary*, March 1997.

_____, *The Great Wall of China, From History to Myth*, Cambridge, U.K.: Cambridge University Press, 1990.

Wang, James C. F., *Contemporary Chinese Politics*, Englewood Cliffs, N.J.: Prentice Hall, 1995.

Wang Jisi, "Comparing Chinese and American Conceptions of Security," draft of paper presented at the NPCSD Workshop on History, Culture and the Prospects of Multilateralism, Beijing, June 7–9, 1992.

_____, "International Relations Theory and the Study of Chinese Foreign Policy: A Chinese Perspective," in Thomas W. Robinson and David Shambaugh, eds., *Chinese Foreign Policy: Theory and Practice*, Oxford: Clarendon Press, 1994.

_____, "Pragmatic Nationalism: China Seeks a New Role in World Affairs," *Oxford International Review*, Winter 1994.

_____, "'Ezhi' haishi 'jiaowang'?: Ping lengzhanhou Meiguo dui Hua zhengce" ["'Containment' or 'Engagement'?: Reviewing post–Cold-War US policy towards China"], *Guoji Wenti Yanjiu [International Studies]*, January 1996.

_____, "The Role of the United States as a Global and Pacific Power," *The Pacific Review*, Vol. 10, No. 1, 1997.

The Washington Times, "China Top Illicit Supplier to Iran, Iraq, Navy Finds," September 2, 1997.

Whiting, Allen, "Assertive Nationalism in Chinese Foreign Policy," *Asian Survey*, August 1993.

_____, *China Crosses the Yalu: The Decision to Enter the Korean War*, New York: Macmillan Company, 1960.

_____, *The Chinese Calculus of Deterrence: India and Indochina*, Ann Arbor: University of Michigan Press, 1975.

Wich, Richard, *Sino-Soviet Crisis Politics: A Study of Political Change and Communication*, Cambridge, Mass.: Harvard University Press, 1980.

Wolf, Charles Jr., K. C. Yeh, Anil Bamezai, Donald P. Henry, and Michael Kennedy, *Long-Term Economic and Military Trends 1994–2015: The United States and Asia,* Santa Monica, Calif.: RAND, MR-627-OSD, 1995.

Womack, Brantly, ed., *Contemporary Chinese Politics in Historical Perspective,* Cambridge, U.K.: Cambridge University Press, 1991.

The World Bank, *China 2020: Development Challenges in the New Century,* Washington, D.C., 1997.

_____, *Sharing Rising Incomes: Disparities in China,* Washington, D.C., 1997.

Wortzel, Larry M., *The ASEAN Regional Forum: Asian Security without an American Umbrella,* Carlisle Barracks, Penn.: U.S. Army War College, 1995.

Wu Xinbo, "Time for the U.S. Military to Leave East Asia," *China Daily,* March 19, 1997.

Yahuda, Michael B., *China's Role in World Affairs,* New York: St. Martin's Press, 1978.

Yao Yunzhu, "Differences Between Western and Chinese Deterrence Theories," paper prepared for Academy of Military Science, People's Liberation Army, China.

Yaomohua zhongguo de beihou [Behind the Demonization of China], Beijing: Shehui Kexue Chubanshe, 1996.

Yu Liqian, Gao Yanfang, and Gao Aisu, "A PLA 'Antibiological Warfare' Unit," *Jiefangjun Bao,* October 21, 1994 in FBIS-China, October 21, 1994.

Yung, C. D., *People's War at Sea: Chinese Naval Power in the Twenty-first Century,* Alexandria, Va.: Center for Naval Analyses, CRM 95-214, 1996.

Zabarenko, Deborah, "Evidence for Chemicals on Ship, U.S. Official Says," *Reuters,* September 7, 1993.

Zaloga, S. J., "Sovremenny: The Instrument of Eastern Power Projection," *Jane's Intelligence Review,* December 1997.

Zang Xiaowei, "Elite Formation and the Bureaucratic-Technocracy in Post-Mao China," *Studies in Comparative Communism,* Vol. 24, No. 1, March 1991.

Zhang Changtai, "It Would be Hard for the Indian Government to Get out of Its Dilemma by Conducting Nuclear Tests," *Jiefangjun Bao* [PLA Daily], May 20, 1998, p. 5, in FBIS-CHI-98-140, 1998.

Zhang, Shu Guang, *Deterrence and Strategic Culture: Chinese-American Confrontations, 1949–1958,* Ithaca, N.Y.: Cornell University Press, 1992.

Zhu Fengqi and Huang Chuangxin, "China's Anti-Chemical Warfare Corps Already Possess a Whole Set of Anti-Nuclear and Anti-Chemical Technology and Equipment," *Zhongguo Xinwen She,* July 13, 1997 in BBC Summary of World Broadcasts, July 22, 1997.